Juan Carlos Scannone SJ

THE GOSPEL OF MERCY IN THE SPIRIT OF DISCERNMENT

Pope Francis' Social Ethics

LIBERIA EDITRICE VATICANA

Published in Australia by

© Copyright 2019 Coventry Press

Coventry Press
33 Scoresby Road
Bayswater Vic. 3153
Australia

Original title: *El Evangelio de la Misericorida en espiritu de discernimiento. La etica social del papa Francisco*

Traduzione dallo spagnolo do Guilia Tura
Translated into English by Salesians Of Don Bosco of the Province of Mary Help Of Christians of Australia and The Pacific

ISBN 9780987643162

© Copyright 2017 - Libreria Editrice Vaticana
00120 Città del Vaticano
Tel. 06.698.81032 - Fax 06.698.84716
commerciale.lev@spc.va

All rights reserved. Other than for the purposes and subject to the conditions prescribed under the *Copyright Act*, no part of this publication may be reproduced, stored in a retrieval system, or transmitted in any form or by any means, electronic, mechanical, photocopying, recording or otherwise, without the prior permission of the publisher.

Cataloguing-in-Publication entry is available from the National Library of Australia http:/catalogue.nla.gov.au/.

Printed in Australia

www.coventrypress.com.au

SERIES
THE THEOLOGY OF POPE FRANCIS

JURGEN WERBICK: *God's weakness for humankind.* Pope Francis' view of God

LUCIO CASULA: *Faces, gestures and places.* Pope Francis' Christology

PETER HÜNERMANN: *Human beings according to Christ today.* Pope Francis' Anthropology

ROBERTO REPOLE: *The dream of a gospel-inspired Church.* Pope Francis' Ecclesiology

CARLOS GALLI: *Christ, Mary, the Church and the peoples.* Pope Francis' Mariology

SANTIAGO MADRIGAL TERRAZAS: *'Unity Prevails over Conflict'.* Pope Francis' Ecumenism

ARISTIDE FUMAGALLI: *Journeying in love.* Pope Francis' Moral Theology

JUAN CARLOS SCANNONE: *The Gospel of Mercy in the spirit of discernment.* Pope Francis' Social Ethics

MARINELLA PERRONI: *Kerygma and prophecy.* Pope Francis' Biblical Hermeneutics

PIERO CODA: *'The Church is the Gospel'.* At the sources of Pope Francis' theology

MARKO IVAN RUPNIK: *According to the Spirit.* Spiritual theology on the move with Pope Francis' Church

ABBREVIATIONS

AL	*Amoris Laetitia*
CV	*Caritas in Veritate*
EG	*Evangelii Gaudium*
EN	*Evangelii Nuntiandi*
GS	*Gaudium et Spes*
LE	*Laborem Exercens*
LF	*Lumen Fidei*
LG	*Lumen Gentium*
LS	*Laudato Si'*
MeM	*Misericordia et Misera*
MM	*Mater et Magistra*
MV	*Misericordiae Vultus*
PP	*Populorum Progressio*
R1	Francis, Holy Father's address to participants in the World Meeting of Popular Movements, Old Hall of the Synod, Tuesday 28 October 2014
R2	Francis, Holy Father's address to participants in the World Meeting of Popular Movements, Paul VI Hall, Saturday 5 November 2016.
SCS	Francis, Holy Father's address to participants in the World Meeting of Popular Movements, Expo Feria, Santa Cruz de la Sierra (Bolivia), Thursday 9 July 2015.

PREFACE TO THE SERIES

From the time of his first appearance in St Peter's Square on the evening of his election, it was more than clear that Francis' pontificate would be adopting a new style. His modest apparel, calling himself the Bishop of Rome, asking the people to pray for him – in the 'deafening silence' of a packed square – and greeting them with a simple '*buonasera*' (good evening) … these were all eloquent signs of the fact that there was a change taking place in the way the Pope related to people, and thus in the 'language' used.

The gestures and words that have followed from that occasion only confirm and strengthen this first impression. Indeed, it could be said that over the ensuing years, the image of the papacy has been decidedly transformed, involving a change that affects homilies, addresses and documents promulgated as well.

As could be predicted, this has generated divergent opinions, especially regarding his teaching. While many have in fact welcomes his magisterium with enthusiasm and deep interest, sensing the fresh wind of the gospel, some others have approached it in a more detached way and, at times, with suspicion. There has been no lack of more absolute views, even going as far as to doubt the existence of a theology in Francis' teaching.

A summary judgement of this kind could come from the very different backgrounds of Francis and his predecessor, Benedict XVI. The latter, we know, has been one of the most outstanding and important theologians of the twentieth century and undoubtedly relied on his personal theological development in his rich papal magisterium. We have not yet fully appreciated, nor will we cease to appreciate, the depth of this magisterium. What Bergoglio has behind him, on the other hand, is his long and deep-rooted experience as a religious and a pastor.

However, this does not mean that his magisterium is without a theology. The fact that he was not mostly, or only, a 'professional' theologian does not mean that his magisterium is not supported by a theology. Were this the case, we could say that, strictly speaking, the majority of his predecessors were without a theology, given that Ratzinger represents the exception rather than the rule.

In any case, the fact that we can discuss the theological significance of Francis' magisterium, as well as the fact that, very often, some of his highly evocative and very immediate expressions have been so abused as to rob them of their profundity – in the journalistic as well as the ecclesial ambit – makes the response of this series, which I have the honour of presenting, a significant one.

By drawing on the competence and rigorous study of theologians of proven worth, coming from diverse contexts, the series has sought to research the theological thinking which supports the Pope's teaching. It explores its roots, its freshness, and its continuity with earlier magisterium.

The result can be found in the eleven volumes which make up this series with its simple and direct title: 'The Theology of Pope Francis'.

They can be read independently of one another, obviously; they have been written by individual authors independently of each other. Nevertheless, the hope is that a reading of the entire series would not only be a valuable aid for grasping the theology upon which Francis' teaching is based, in the various theological fields of knowledge, but also an introduction to the key points of his thinking and teaching overall.

The intention, then, is not one of 'apologetics', and even less so is it to add further voices to the many already speaking about the Pope. The aim is to try to see, and to help others to see, what theological thinking Francis bases himself on and expresses, in such a fresh way in his teaching.

Among the many discoveries the reader could make in reading these volumes, would certainly be that of observing how so much of the beneficial freshness of the Council's teaching flows into Francis' magisterium. This is true both of the theological preparation he has had, and of what has followed from it. Given that it is perhaps still too soon for all this wealth to become common patrimony, peacefully and fully received by everyone, it should be no surprise that the Pope's teaching is sometimes not immediately understood by everyone.

By the same token, a point of no return has been reached in Francis' teaching, one that recent theology and the Council have both taught: that doctrine cannot be something extraneous to so-called pastoral theology and ministry. The truth that the Church is called to watch over is the truth of Christ's gospel, which needs to be communicated to the women and men of every time and place. This is why the task of the ecclesial magisterium must also be one of favouring this communication of the Gospel. Hence, theology can never be reduced to a dry, desk-bound exercise, disconnected from the life of the people of God and its mission. This mission is that the women and men of every age encounter the perennial and inexhaustible freshness of Jesus' gospel.

Over these years there have been those who have heard some of Francis' own critical statements regarding theology or theologians, and have concluded that he holds it and them in low esteem. Perhaps a more detailed study of the Pope's teaching, such as offered by this series, could also be helpful for showing that, while we always need to be critical of a theology that loses its vital connection to the living faith of the Church, it is also essential to have a theology which takes up the task of thinking critically about this very faith, and doing so with 'creative fidelity', so that it may continue to be proclaimed.

Francis' teaching is certainly not lacking in a theology of this kind; and a theology of the kind is certainly one much desired by a magisterium such as his, which so wants God's mercy to continue to touch the minds and hearts of the women and men of our time.

Editor-in-chief
ROBERTO REPOLE

CONTENTS

Abbreviations 4
Preface to the Series 5
Introduction 15

Part 1
The Good News of mercy

Chapter 1
The key thread of mercy 21

Part 2
Preferential, caring option for the poor

Chapter 1
'A poor church for the poor' 31

1. Recent history 32
2. The essential nature of the social
   dimension of evangelization 34
3. The social dimension of evangelization 37
   3.1. Inclusion of the poor in society 38
   3.2. An economic system 'that kills' 47
   3.3. Cultural challenges 51

Chapter 2

The socially active role of the poor and outcast 53

1. *Kairos in the crisis situation.* 55
2. *Actors, poets and those who make history* 56
3. *Toward authentic democracy* 59
4. *Tasks for constructing the common good* 60
   4.1. The three 'L's (in Spanish, the three 't's) 61
   4.2. Other connected problems 65
5. *The mysticism which gives energy to the process* 68
6. *The Church's contribution* 71

Chapter 3

Care for our common home 74

1. *The current Pope's first Encyclical* 74
2. *See' 'what is happening to our common home' (LS, no. 17 ff.)* 78
3. *Theology of creation* 81
4. *The common destination of goods* 83
5. *The technocratic paradigm* 85
6. *Ecology and anthropology* 92
7. *Toward an integral ecology* 94
8. *The common good* 98
9. *Dialogue for a culture of encounter* 102
   9.1. At the international level 102

- 9.2. National and local levels 105
- 9.3. Politics and economy in dialogue for human fulfilment ... 107
- 9.4. Dialogue between religions and science 109
- 9.5. Spirituality, education and ecological conversion 111
- 9.6. The fruits of Christian spirituality and its trinitarian foundation 116

PART 3
Ecclesial and personal discernment

CHAPTER 1

DISCERNING GOD'S SIGNS IN PERSONAL AND WORLD HISTORY 121

1. *Ecclesial discernment of the signs of the times* 123
2. *Analogy with Ignatian discernment at a personal level* 125
3. *Analogical shift from the personal to the social* 136
4. *Four principles as criteria for discernment* .. 141
    - 4.1. Time and space 142
    - 4.2. Unity prevails over conflict 145
    - 4.3. Realities are more important than ideas 149

4.4. The whole is greater than the part (and the mere sum of its parts) ...151

4.5. Toward a succinct view of the four principles 155

INTRODUCTION

Faced with the challenge of briefly presenting Pope Francis' social ethics, it seemed to me that the only thing we could do was to begin from the so genuinely evangelical and typical Bergoglian theme of *mercy*. Then from there, it would seem to be easy enough to recognize many of the key approaches, ideas, writings, attitudes and gestures which characterize his pontificate, especially his pastoral and social theology, and which the people of God of the 21st century have been able to perceive and appreciate.

One of the immediate consequences of this approach leads to the *preferential option for the poor* which, from Medellín to Aparecida, emerged explicitly formulated thus – in the Latin American Church. It was then recognized by the universal magisterium of the popes who have been Bergoglio's immediate predecessors. From the outset, he has expressed his wish for 'a poor Church for the poor,' considering the poor not only as beneficiaries but also as protagonists in today's global peaceful struggle for complete freedom. Today, among the most vulnerable of the vulnerable, meaning among the 'poor', we also include our 'sister, mother Earth,' such that we are currently immersed in not two but only *one* social and environmental crisis to which the Pope dedicated his first Encyclical. It challenges us to make historically effective choices of mercy for the *life* of the poor and the Earth.

Yet, since we are not only talking about the basic contents of social ethics but also of his *method*, a third step is needed so we can understand how Francis develops and presents it. What sets it apart is the practice (and the teaching) of *discernment* of spirits and especially the presence and action of the Holy Spirit who brings us to a knowledge of the Father's will in Christ. I am convinced that such discernment helps him to lead and govern the 21st century Church and its missionary conversion to a Church which goes forth into the globalized world in crisis. He not only carries out this discernment himself, but teaches it to the faithful and to pastors, even in very difficult situations, such as the case of the divorced and remarried – a sorrowful sign of the times in our secularized West which needs to be tackled with truth and mercy.

It seemed to me to be an acceptable approach for this work to follow the golden thread of mercy in all this, with its subsequent steps of preferential option for the poor and spiritual discernment, including the ecclesial interpretation of the signs of the times which Vatican Council II demanded of the Church. I then consider that other key themes of Bergoglio's, such as the joy of the Gospel, the revolution of tenderness, a non-inwardly focused Church, the Church going forth, missionary conversion, going out to the peripheries, as also the different approaches of his theology and his social and pastoral ethics concerning family, culture, economy, politics, ecology etc., will flow from the three points chosen and/or intertwine with them.

This is why, to present the theme of this work as set out in the subtitle, and with the interpretative focus I have given it, I chose: 'The Gospel of Mercy in the spirit of discernment' to be the main title. Francis' social ethics come from the gospel, whose substance – according to him – is nothing if not mercy (hence the priority the poor have) and it is exercised in a spirit of discernment, which is itself evangelical. The word 'Spirit' could have been capitalized in the title to allude to the fact that Bergoglio's social ethics have a trinitarian, christological and pneumatological focus, given that the first source of mercy is the Father, who is revealed in the gospel of the Son – both for the Church in its social doctrine and for each member of the faithful – in the light of the Spirit, and is put into practice thanks to the power of this gift.

As a consequence, the first part of this work will tackle the fundamental and basic problem of divine *mercy* and its human reflection in those who allow themselves to be moved to act in this spirit (first chapter). The second part will be dedicated to the *option for the poor*, subdivided into three sections, namely, a reference to the 'Church of the poor' (John XXIII, Cardinal Lercaro) and 'poor for the poor' (second chapter); another chapter will deal with the part played by popular movements in the struggle for what in Spanish are the three 't's and in English the three 'l's: *tierra*=land, *techo*=lodging, *trabajo*=labour, taking my inspiration from Francis' addresses to these popular movements (third chapter). The third section of the second part will focus on our sister, Mother Earth, embracing the great majority of its inhabitants, the poor, and I will then comment on the Pope's Encyclical regarding an integral or socio-environmental ecology (fourth chapter). Finally, the last part of the book will deal with ecclesial and personal *discernment* of spirits, especially of The Spirit, because, through the method employed by the Church's social doctrine ('see, judge, act') this last part throws light on the trinitarian aspect of the practice of mercy which preferentially opts for the poor (fifth chapter).

Within these three broad frames of reference I will be cobbling together the various contributions Francis makes to the Church's social teaching and ethics.

Part 1

The Good News of Mercy

Chapter 1
THE KEY THREAD OF MERCY

When Jesuit Fr Jorge Mario Bergoglio was appointed bishop, he chose as his episcopal motto the line from St Bede the Venerable, '*miserando atque eligendo*' saying that 'Jesus looked upon Matthew with merciful love and chose him' (*MV* no. 8). Francis says 'this expression impressed me so much' (*ibid.*) that he felt it involved him personally, so much so that he retained it as the motto for his pontificate. More than it being just a statement, I believe we are dealing with a charism, an existential spirit and mood, a living doctrine, a way of governing. While recognizing that he is a sinner, he accepts that he has been chosen out of pure, freely offered mercy, and hence called to the mission of living, practising and teaching it: 'a sinner, but also a minister of mercy' (*MeM*, no. 10).

One could say that his social ethics, his recovery of the social dimension of the gospel from the sources, thus continuing the Church's social magisterium, renews itself and continues to flow from this stream of living water. We could apply to the Holy Father himself what he says in general: 'I am loved therefore I exist; I am forgiven therefore I am reborn; I have been shown mercy therefore I have become a vessel of mercy' (*MeM*, no. 16), which is a 'wellspring of joy, serenity and peace' (*MV*, no. 2; cf. *MeM*, no. 3), namely, a wellspring of the joy of the gospel.

This is where the Pope encounters 'the very substance' (letter to Poli), 'the core' (*MV*, no. 9), the 'key word' (*ibid.*), the 'summing up' (*MV*, no. 1), the 'fundamental law' (*MV*, no. 2), the 'very foundation' (*MV*, no. 10) of the Good News of Jesus, 'the word [which] reveals the very mystery of the Most Holy Trinity' and 'the bridge that connects God and man' (*MV*, no.2) since according to Francis, 'from the heart of the Trinity, from the depths of the mystery of God, the great river of mercy wells up and overflows unceasingly' (*MV*, no. 25). The Argentinian theologian, Carlos Maria Galli, goes as far as to say: 'Mercy is the principle hermeneutic of Francis' pontificate.'[1] We note that he does not speak only of his theology, but of his papacy as a whole. It is no coincidence that Francis' first trip outside Rome was to Lampedusa, a grand gesture to the future which symbolizes this decisive key to interpretation.

So Christ – in the light of the Spirit – *is* the 'face of the mercy' (*misericordiae vultus*) of the Father whose 'most stupendous attribute' (*DM*, no. 13; *MV*, no. 11) consists precisely of his mercy, according to St John Paul II, which 'rather than a sign of weakness, is the mark of his omnipotence' (MV, no. 6). So, one cannot doubt that mercy has trinitarian roots for Francis, roots in which the social dimension of the gospel is ultimately based (*EG*, no. 176). Or in other words, in the Father's infinite love which confers an infinite dignity on every man and woman (*EG*, no. 178)

---

1 Cf. CM Galli, 'Líneas teológicas, pastorales y espirituales del Magisterio del Papa Francisco', *Medellín* 33 (2017), 93-158, 105.

through the redemptive blood of the Son who 'redeems not only the individual person, but also the social relations existing between men' (*ibid.*) and through the revitalizing action of the Holy Spirit who is 'at work in everyone', 'to penetrate every human situation and all social bonds', and 'knows how to loosen the knots of human affairs, even the most complex and inscrutable' (*ibid.*). Hence 'the very mystery of the Trinity reminds us that we have been created in the image of that divine communion, and so we cannot achieve fulfillment or salvation purely by our own efforts' (*ibid.*), but as the faithful People of God and his kingdom (*EG*, no. 176).

However, mercy does not only correspond to the very substance of the gospel, with its roots in the Triune God who is merciful Love, but is in line with one of the most typical needs of our time. As I will say further on, our world is suffering a profound socio-environmental crisis without precedent (cf. *EG* and *LS*). The poor and the earth are crying out to heaven and demanding both justice and compassion of us, not only toward those who suffer from this crisis, but also because of the personal, social and structural sin of those who cause this suffering.

'This is the time of mercy,' the Holy Father repeated at the conclusion of the Jubilee Year, following on from John XXIII and the Council in this when the good Pope said: 'Now the Bride of Christ wishes to use the medicine of mercy rather than taking up arms of severity' (*MV*, no. 4, quoting *Gaudet Mater Ecclesia*). So, if we are in crisis 'at the end of the modern era'[2], and this requires a new evangelization – proclaimed by St John Paul II – as well as the corresponding pastoral and missionary conversion of the Church – advocated at Aparecida by Latin America – we not only need the Lord's mercy (he is always ready to show it), and his Church's mercy as we undergo this crisis, but need also to show mercy to one another. Peoples should show mercy to other peoples, especially to the poor and victims of history, but also to the perpetrators that they may be converted. The Pontiff specifies that 'in the present day, as the Church is charged with the task of the new evangelization, the theme of mercy needs to be proposed again and again with new enthusiasm and renewed pastoral action' (*MV*, no. 12).

As a consequence, mere theorizing 'about' mercy is not enough (*MeM*, no. 20), but 'wherever there are Christians everyone should find an oasis of mercy' (*MV*, no. 12) given that as followers of Jesus 'we are called to create a *culture of mercy*' (*MeM*, no. 20) to 'set in motion a real cultural revolution' (*ibid.*). In other texts, the Holy Father calls it the 'revolution of tenderness' (*EN*, no. 88) which starts with the heart and changes the mentality of societies and peoples, transforming both their culture and their institutions and structures.

Francis asserts that Jesus not only preaches a change of personal relationships with God and others but also with his Father's Kingdom, a social and public reign of 'universal fraternity, justice, peace and dignity' (*EG*, no. 180). His

---

2   Cf. R GUARDINI *Das Ende der Neuzeit*, Würzburg, 1965, cited in LS 105, note 83, etc.

'principle of discernment' is universality, which Paul VI applied to development: 'directed to all men and the whole man' (*PP*, no. 14), that is, 'all dimensions of existence, all individuals, all areas of community life, and all peoples' (*EG*, no. 181).

An evangelizing community, then, 'has an endless desire to show mercy, the fruit of its own experience of the power of the Father's infinite mercy' (*EG*, no. 24). It 'can move forward, boldly take the initiative, go out to others, seek those who have fallen away, stand at the crossroads, and welcome the outcast' because 'the Lord has taken the initiative, he has loved us first (cf. Jn 4:10)' (*ibid.*). Divine mercy is thus the source of mercy for each Christian and for the ecclesial community. That is how, for example, the post-synodal Exhortation, *Amoris Laetitia,* transmits not only the joy of love but also the benevolent understanding of the circumstances of many marriages in an 'irregular situation' (*AL*, Ch. 8), the compassion and forgiveness of God.

In his Apostolic Letter *Misericordia et Misera* (*MeM*, no. 1), the Pope contemplates, with St Augustine, the encounter between Jesus, 'the face of the Father's mercy', and the poor sinner who represents each of us, himself included, since he frequently declares himself a sinner, as a reason for opening our hearts to mercy and reconciliation with our fellow sinners and sufferers, allowing ourselves 'to be deeply moved' (*EG*, no. 193) with a 'visceral love' (*MV*, no. 6) and therefore knowable from experience, very concrete and effective. This is how 'the profound truths of the Gospel are made manifest and tangible' (*MeM*, no. 1). They become 'the most visible sign of the Father's love' (*MeM*, no. 2) in a kind of phenomenology of faith which many non-believers also know how to interpret.

However, as we have said, we are not only talking about an interpersonal, face-to-face between Divine Mercy and human misery in brief relations (Paul Ricoeur) but also broader relations, those of reconciliation and peace among peoples and groups fighting among themselves within the same people, such as is the case in Syria or Colombia. The Pope gives special attention to these.

It is clear that mercy does not replace justice but presumes it and surpasses it, preventing it from falling into 'legalism by distorting the original meaning of justice and obscuring its profound value' (*MV*, no. 20). Following these words, the Pope shows how Jesus and following him, Paul, overcome the legalistic perspective of the Pharisees of their day, ultimately concluding: 'God's justice is his mercy' (cf. Ps 51:11-16)' (*ibid.*).

'Mere justice is not enough. Experience shows that an appeal to justice alone will result in its destruction' (*MV*, no. 21) says the Pope. And almost immediately he adds: 'God does not deny justice. He rather envelops it and surpasses it with an even greater event in which we experience love as the foundation of true justice' (*ibid.*). Well then, this event is mercy faced with the misery of the sinner. We cannot place conditions on it, since 'it is always a gratuitous act of our heavenly Father, an unconditional and unmerited act of love' (*MeM*, no. 12). Furthermore, in the Church's prayer it is 'highly *performative*, which is to say that as we invoke mercy with faith, it is granted to us' (*MeM*, no. 5). According to Jon Sobrino, the first and last way of describing mercy - for God, Christ and for the human being – is for it to be exercised. Only this fully explains it[3] and is a gift of mercy itself.

As a conclusion to this first chapter, we could say that Pope Francis' social ethics and his contribution to the Church's social doctrine are radically theological because they come from the heart of the Trinity itself, are focused on Christ and the following of Christ and are put together according to the theological rhythm of mercy which includes not only brief personal interrelationships ('micro-relations', *CV*, no. 2): with God, between people and with nature, but also broader relationships: cultural, political, social, economic ('macro-relations', *ibid.*) especially with the most wretched, be it for their poverty, exclusion and/or discrimination, or for their individual or structural sin. Hence the first approach of this book, focused on mercy, flows obviously into the second: the merciful option for the poor by a poor Church of, with and for the poor.

---

3   Cf. J Sobrino, 'Hacer teología en América Latina' (Doing theology in America), *Theologica Xaveriana* 39 (1989), 139-156, 145.

Part 2

Preferential, caring option for the poor

Chapter 1
'A POOR CHURCH FOR THE POOR'

According to Francis, the reality is viewed better and more completely from the periphery, not from the centre. So that is where he situates himself, from the point of view of the least and the poor, to consider today's world, the crisis it is going through, and the response which the Church must give through its missionary conversion, and which all of humankind should give through their communal, socio-ecological conversion, moved and motivated by mercy shown 'from above'.

This chapter will first of all briefly present the history of this perspective from just prior to the Second Vatican Council. It will then pick up once more what was said in the previous chapter on the essential nature of the gospel's social dimension, with a view to providing a solid foundation for the two points to follow. Then it will spend time with the current situation, where civilization is in crisis, a global threat which we need to respond to without delay. Finally, it will specify what Francis' proposal is, in the face of this challenge, a proposal addressed to humankind as a whole – 'to all men and women of good will' (*LS*, no. 3) – and especially to the Church.

1. Recent history

In my opinion, Pope Francis is carrying out the unfinished agenda of Vatican II (1962-1965) in this regard. Shortly before opening it, St John XXIII said: 'Faced with poor countries, the Church presents itself as it is and as it would like to be: a Church for everyone, but especially the Church of the poor.'[1]

Then later, during the Council, Cardinal Giacomo Lercaro, Archbishop of Bologna, proposed that '*the* great theme of the Council' was 'the Church ... in that it is, *essentially*, the Church of the poor' (italics mine). This intervention had a strong impact. The theme was taken into account and some of the Council Fathers met separately to deal with it, many of them signing the so-called Pact of the Catacombs, promoted by Dom Helder Camara among others.[2] Nevertheless, what Vatican II Church historian, Giuseppe Alberigo, said later about the Council continues to hold true, viz., that the principal omission of the Council was its commitment to poor peoples, as John XXIII had asked for, and to the Church's own poverty.[3]

Later it was the Latin American Church – as a new 'Church source' – which responded to this challenge and

---

1 Cf. JOHN XXIII, Radio message, 11 September 1962.
2 See the text in English at http://www.pactofthecatacombs.com/the-document.
3 Cf. G ALBERIGO, *Breve historia del Concilio Vaticano II. En busca de la renovación del cristianesimo*, Salamanca, Síguemi, 2005, 195 ff. Also available in English as *A Brief History of Vatican II* (Trans. Matthew Sherry), Orbis Books, Maryknoll, New York, 2006

which now the Pope, who has 'come from the end of the Earth' and from this tradition, wants to 'put at the centre of the Church's pilgrim way' (*EG*, no. 198), and at the heart of the new evangelization and the missionary and pastoral conversion this implies. This is confirmed by the history of the General Conferences of the Latin American and Caribbean Bishops at Medellín (1968)[4] and Aparecida (2007),[5] the latter's concluding document having been guided by Bergoglio. Hence, we can better rediscover the reality from the periphery and its perspective, that of the centrality of the poor in Jesus' message, the inhuman situation experienced by the majority of the world's poor today 'in an era of globalization and exclusion,' and that of 'our common home,' our Sister, Mother Earth.

2. *The essential nature of the social dimension of evangelization*

Chapter 4 of his road map, *Evangelii Gaudium*, written to point out 'new paths for the Church's journey in years to come' (*EG*, no. 1) begins by duly explaining this dimension It begins, as we have already said, from its trinitarian foundation and the core of the *kerygma* or first proclamation of the Good News that God is Love, loves us and saves us as his people. 'The kerygma has a clear social content: at the very heart of the Gospel is life in community and engagement with others' (*EG*, no. 177). From this comes

---

4 SECOND GENERAL CONFERENCE OF THE LATIN AMERICAN EPISCOPATE, Medellín Document, 24 August–5 September, 1968.

5 FIFTH GENERAL CONFERENCE OF THE LATIN AMERICAN EPISCOPATE, Aparecida Document, 13–31 May, 2007.

the recognition not only of 'the profound connection between evangelization and human advancement' (*EG*, no. 178, alluding to *EN*, no. 31), but also the recognition that 'the service of charity is also a constituent element of the Church's mission and an indispensable expression of her very being' (*EG*, no. 179, quoting Benedict XVI).

It should be noted that after the 1971 Synod on Justice, which taught that the struggle for justice is a *constituent element* of evangelization, there was discussion at both the 1974 Synod on Evangelization and at the Puebla Conference (1979) as to whether it was the case of being an *essential* constituent or only an *integral* one. If it is the former, without the social dimension there is no true evangelization: not if evangelization is limited to the merely religious and cultural. St John Paul II, in his first Encyclical *Redemptor Hominis* no. 15, described it as essential – restating this later in *Centesimus Annus* no. 5 – as it would also appear to be in the citation from Benedict employed by Francis (cf. *EG*, no. 179). This is not the point on which he begins to differ from his predecessors, but he does so especially by going into much more concrete circumstances.

The current Pontiff recognizes that 'the Church's teaching concerning contingent situations … can be open to discussion,' but adds 'we cannot help but be concrete – without presuming to enter into details – lest the great social principles remain mere generalities which challenge no one. There is a need to draw practical conclusions, so that they 'will have greater impact …' (*EG*, no. 182, quoting the *Compendium of the Social Doctrine of the Church*, no. 9). Not for nothing did Benedict XVI emeritus call Francis 'the man of practical reform.'

Nevertheless, Francis does so 'without presuming to enter into details' (*EG*, no. 182), since 'it is not the task of the Pope to offer a detailed and complete analysis of contemporary reality' (EG, no. 51); but – as I will explain especially in Part Three of this work – he not only discerns the signs of the times in the light of faith, but also encourages Christian communities to do likewise (*ibid.*). Further on he states that 'neither the Pope nor the Church has a monopoly on the interpretation of social realities or the proposal of solutions to contemporary problems' (*EG*, no. 184). And he recalls Paul VI's observation that 'in the face of such widely varying situations, it is difficult ... to put forward a solution which has universal validity'; but 'it is up to the Christian communities to analyze with objectivity the situation which is proper to their own country' (*ibid.*, quoting *Octogesima Adveniens*, no. 4).

Consequently, if we follow the method St John XXIII applies to the Church's social doctrine: 'See, judge, act' (*Mater et Magistra*, no. 236), 'The Church's pastors, taking into account the contributions of the different sciences, have the right to offer opinions on all that affects people's lives,' since' God wants his children to be happy in this world too' (*EG*, no. 182), having 'created all things "for our enjoyment" (1 Tim 6:17), the enjoyment of *everyone*' (*ibid.*). I need to note in passing that he talks about pastors *as* pastors and not just as citizens. Furthermore, I note that the Pope recommends – for the pastoral 'seeing' that is faith – the use of corresponding sciences as intermediaries, and that his understanding is still historically, not just eschatologically positive, since he combines the happiness of God's children on this earth with the joy of the gospel.

So 'it is no longer possible to claim that religion should be restricted to the private sphere' (*EG*, no. 182) 'without influence on societal and national life, without concern for the soundness of civil institutions, without a right to offer an opinion on events affecting society' (*EG*, no. 183). 'If indeed 'the first ordering of society and of the state is a central responsibility of politics', the Church cannot and must not remain on the sidelines in the fight for justice" (*ibid*., quoting *Deus Caritas Est*, no. 28). 'All Christians, their pastors included, are called to show concern for the building of a better world' (*EG*, no. 183). This is what the Pope is attempting to do, without claiming to have the solution but trying to offer an effective contribution to the common good.

3. *The social dimension of evangelization*

According to Carlos Galli, mentioned earlier, nos. 186–216 of *Evangelii Gaudium* 'is the most significant text a Pope has written in twenty centuries on Christ, the Church and the poor.'[6] These paragraphs shape the second section of Chapter 4 of the Exhortation, immediately preceded by the

---

6 Cf. 'La reforma de la Iglesia impulsada por Francisco' (The reform of the Church driven by Francis). Dialogue with Carlos María Galli, Dean of the Faculty of Theology at the Pontifical Argentine Catholic University, in *Vida Nueva* (Madrid), No. 3026 (4-10 March 2017), Pliego, 1-8, 7.

first section which serves as a general introduction to the whole chapter.

I have already presented much of the contribution of this first section by referring both to mercy and human advancement as the *essential* constituent elements of evangelization. He not only bases the social dimension on the core of the *kerygma* and key texts of Old and New Testaments, but also points to the essential trinitarian component of the issue, as also its public nature, including at national and international levels. He then refers in general to the Church's social teaching and its *Compendium* in order to focus solely on 'two great issues which strike me as fundamental at this time in history,' namely, 'the inclusion of the poor in society' (the section to which Galli alludes in the quotation above) and 'peace and social dialogue' (*EG*, no. 185).

3.1 Inclusion of the poor in society

When the Medellín Conference (1968) interpreted the signs of the times in order to apply Vatican II to Latin America, what stood out among other things was the reality of the structurally unjust poverty in a continent the majority of which was Catholic. Such a serious situation was then read in the light not only of the Council, but also of the Encyclical *Populorum Progessio* (1967) by Paul VI, especially his *integral development* (of 'all men and of man as a whole'). This is a Pope whom Bergoglio respects very much. This theme was explored more deeply in the plenary assemblies of the Latin American and Caribbean Bishops Conferences to follow, up to and including Aparecida.

There, Benedict XVI clearly pointed to the *christological* basis of the option for the poor, that is, faith in the God who became poor for us, so as to enrich us with his poverty' (EG, no. 198, quoting the Address at the Inaugural Session).[7] Francis also begins his discussion on 'the inclusion of the poor in society' in *Evangelii Gaudium*, from 'our faith in Christ who became poor, and was always close to the poor and the outcast' (*EG*, no. 186). This becomes the basis for [his] concern for the integral development of society's most neglected members' (*ibid.*).

The Pope then turns to the Sacred Scriptures to hear there 'the cry of the poor' (*EG*, nos. 187. 188), which moves us not only to 'small daily acts of solidarity' (*EG*, no. 188) but also – illustrated in our century by science and experience – working to eliminate the *structural causes* of poverty and to promote the integral development of the poor' (*ibid.*, italics mine). But, according to the Pontiff, in order to succeed there is need for the virtue of solidarity in individuals and in society itself.

St John Paul II had already given enormous importance to this in *Sollicitudo Rei Socialis,* and for Francis it also presumes a *cultural* change regarding current competitive individualism. It means the creation of 'a new mindset which thinks in terms of community and the priority of the life of all over the appropriation of goods by a few' (*EG*, no. 188). Even though a radical transformation of structures is essential, it is not enough 'without generating

7   *AAS* [99] 2007, 450.

new convictions and attitudes', because, without these, new structures 'will become, sooner or later, corrupt, oppressive and ineffectual' (*EG*, no. 189). Hence the need for a sincere recognition, both personal and socio-cultural, of 'the social function of property and the universal destination of goods [as] realities which come before private property' (*ibid.*). Francis thus picks up the classical contributions of the Church's social doctrine. However, given the urgency of the suffering of the majority, he expresses it in a most concrete and comprehensible language and in a tone which asserts its prophetic force.

Today, it is a matter or 'hearing the cry of entire peoples, the poorest peoples of the earth' (*EG*, no. 190), since we need to respect not only 'human rights, but also … The rights of peoples' (*ibid.*). So 'the mere fact that some people are born in places with fewer resources or less development does not justify the fact that they are living with less dignity' (*ibid.*). Later, in his first encyclical, Francis would criticize the fact that we continue 'to tolerate that some consider themselves more human than others, as if they had been born with greater rights' (*LS*, no. 90).

Above all, we are scandalized that there is so much hunger in some places when we know 'that there is enough food for everyone' (*EG*, no. 191). But this 'is the result of a poor distribution of goods and income,' while in other parts of the same country or the planet there is an increase of 'the generalized practice of wastefulness' (*ibid.*). All in all, the Pope's dream is a very lofty one, given that he wants for all people not just a 'dignified sustenance' – which so many lack, nevertheless – but 'their general temporal welfare and prosperity' (*ibid.*, quoting *Mater et Magistra*, no. 3), because, as he has already said, God wants his children to be happy even on earth, consistent with their dignity (cf. *EG*, no. 183).

Then Francis returns to mercy once again, when 'we incarnate the duty of hearing the cry of the poor' and 'are deeply moved' (*EG*, no. 193) thanks to being challenged by the Word of God, as already explained in the previous chapter. Stemming from this is that 'God's heart has a special place for the poor' (*EG*, no. 197) and that 'for the Church, the option for the poor is primarily a *theological category* rather than a cultural, sociological, political or philosophical one' (*EG*, no. 198, italics mine), a detail which sees the current Pope take a more advanced position than his predecessors.

In such an important context, he officially repeats the longing he has expressed since the beginning of his pontificate and which serves as the guide for exercising it: 'This is why I want a Church which is poor and for the poor' (*ibid.*). He explains *why* in a beautiful text to follow which is so from the beginning to the end, so I will quote it in full:

> They have much to teach us. Not only do they share in the *sensus fidei*, but in their difficulties they know the suffering Christ. We need to let ourselves be evangelized by them. The new evangelization is an invitation to acknowledge the saving power at work in their lives and to put them at the centre of the Church's pilgrim way. We are called to find Christ in them, to lend our voice to their causes, but also to be their

> friends, to listen to them, to speak for them and
> to embrace the mysterious wisdom which God
> wishes to share with us through them (*ibid.*)

Just as the Holy Father allowed himself to be evangelized by them, he is now attempting to evangelize the whole Church by beginning from them and the poor Christ and so bring the world the message of the new evangelization directed both to the Churches and nations which received the first proclamation along the way, and to peoples not yet evangelized. So the 'peoples *with* spirit', according to Ignacio Ellacuría, materially poor and at the same time 'people *of* spirit', teach us not only the Good News but also a genuine humanism and popular wisdom which is as human as it is often also Christian. In order to receive it, considering 'the other "in a certain sense as one with ourselves"' (*EG*, no. 199), we need to learn to make them our friends, through friendship and contemplative love which entails 'appreciating the poor in their goodness, in their experience of life, in their culture, and in their ways of living the faith' (*ibid.*), meaning, as I will say further ahead, in their popular piety.

According to Venezuelan theologian, Pedro Trigo, there are at least three possible interpretations of the expression 'Church of the poor' as employed by Pope John and by Lercaro, which he compares with Francis' use of the term. They are: 1) that the Church *without* being poor, considers them as the *preferred beneficiaries* of its activity; 2) where they find themselves 'at home' in the Church; 3) and in addition, where they are the privileged active subjects of its life and mission,[8] that is to say, they are the *heart* of the Church and its practice. The first interpretation is excluded in Bergoglio's case if we bear in mind his wish for a *poor* Church, not only one *for* the poor. The second coincides with what the Pope says in *Evangelii Gaudium*, no. 199, when he says, citing *Novo Millennio Ineunte*, no. 50: 'that the poor in each Christian community may feel at home.' Thanks be to God, I believe this is already happening in many local Churches in various regions around the planet: there, the Church is a setting which the poor can consider their own, along with those who are not poor.

However, we lack a true *spiritual, pastoral and structural* conversion to the poor Christ and to the poor to realize the third interpretation of the term, which the Pope explains as putting them 'at the *centre* of the Church's pilgrim way' (*EG*, no. 198; italics mine), meaning at the heart of the Church as communion in the Spirit, an evangelizing community and institution. The active role of the poor and outcast in society as 'privileged active subjects' (Trigo), is recognized by Francis in his different addresses to popular movements. They are still not 'at the centre of society nor of the Church.'

As already quoted, the Holy Father exhorts us to also value the poor for 'their ways of living the faith' (*EG*, no. 199), that is, for their inculturated popular piety. Vatican Council II did not tackle this subject, but it was taken up

---

8 Cf. P Trigo, 'Una Iglesia pobre para los pobres. ¿A dónde nos lleva el sueño del papa Francisco?' (A poor Church for the poor. Where is Pope Francis' dream taking us?), *Revista latinoamericano de Teología* 30 (2013), 247-262.

initially at Medellíin, then by Latin American theology, especially in Argentina (and this issue had a decisive influence on the young Bergoglio) and through the 1974 Synod on Evangelization. Then, more probably through the mediation of the future Cardinal Eduardo Pironio, it was taken up by Paul VI in *Evangelii Nuntiandi* (1975). Puebla studied and applied this Exhortation to Latin America. At Puebla the main editors of the key sections on the evangelization of culture and popular religiosity were Lucio Gera and Joaquín Alliende respectively. The former, much appreciated by Archbishop and Cardinal Bergoglio, was the chief representative of the 'theology of the people' in Argentina,[9] which the latter encouraged from Chile as the 'theology of popular pastoral ministry'. Thus it became a fertile, increasingly back-and-forth discussion from the Latin American periphery ('the end of the earth', 'south of the South') to the centre in Rome and vice versa.

This line of thinking continued in Latin America up to and including Aparecida, which dealt not only with 'popular religiosity' (*Medellín*, no. 6), 'the religion of the people' and/or 'popular piety' (*EN*, no. 48) but likewise with 'spirituality and the people's mysticism' (*Aparecida*, no. 262). As Pope, Francis is heir to this tradition, has universalized it and taken new steps forward in his theological and pastoral assessment of it.

---

9 For the 'theology of the people' I refer you to my books: *Evangelización, cultura y teología*, Buenos Aires, Guadalupe, 1990 (2nd ed., Buenos Aires, Docencia, 2011) and *La teología del pueblo. Raíces teológicas del Papa Francisco*, Santander, Sal Terrae, 2017.

During World Youth Day at Rio de Janeiro, he viewed popular piety in opposition to the temptation to clericalism and an adult creation of the laity among the faithful People.[10] Later, in *Evangelii Gaudium,* he called it, as did *Aparecida*, nos. 262–263, 'popular spirituality' and 'the people's mysticism' (*EG,* no. 124) and 'a spirituality incarnated in the culture of the lowly' (*ibid.*); but then he moved on to consider it 'a *locus theologicus*' which demands our attention, especially at a time when we are looking to the new evangelization' (*EG,* no. 126), recognizing it as a *locus theologicus* in the sense that Melchor Cano understood it, as a *source* for theology. Francis sees it as a key to new evangelization. Finally, further on in the same Exhortation he presents it as embracing the *totality* of the life of faith, stating: 'The genius of each people receives in its own way the entire Gospel and embodies it in expressions of prayer, fraternity, justice, struggle and celebration' (*EG,* no. 237).

This latter Bergoglian formulation of the communal mysticism of the inculturated faithful People of God not only takes into account specific moments in reference to God (prayer and celebration, even when this latter is not always religious), but it also includes an *active* relationship with one's neighbour: fraternity, justice and struggle, to be understood primarily in a positive sense as the struggle for life, justice, peace, and for the common good of everyone in fraternity and justice.

---

10   Cf. Francis, Address to the bishops of CELAM (World Youth Day 2013, Rio de Janeiro), no. 4, point 3.

3.2 An economic system 'that kills'

The other side of the preferential option for the poor and the desire for a poor Church for the poor is affirmation of 'the need to resolve the *structural causes* of poverty' and 'of inequality' (*EG*, no. 202, italics mine). For the Pope, these causes lie especially in 'the *absolute* autonomy of the marketplace and financial speculation (*ibid.*, italics mine)., an autonomy defended by ideologies (which St John Paul II called neo-liberal) 'which reject the right of states, charged with the vigilance for the common good, to exercise any form of control' (*EG*, no. 56).

The Pope, instead, favours politics with regard to the economy, calling it 'one of the highest forms of charity, inasmuch as it seeks the common good' (*EG*, no. 205). For him, as for Benedict XVI, theological charity 'is the principle ... also of macro-relationships (social, economic and political ones)' (*ibid.*, quoting from *Caritas in Veritate*, no. 2). They can all be informed by love, but while economics looks to the most effective *means*, politics looks to the *ends*, summed up in what he called 'the common good' (local, national, international).

It is the *ideologized* because absolutized economic system – and not the socio-economics of the marketplace – which Francis rejects when he criticizes 'the sacralized workings of the prevailing economic system' (*EG*, no. 54), and says 'no' to 'an economy of exclusion and inequality', since 'such an economy kills' (*EG*, no. 53), and 'no to the new idolatry of money', to a 'socioeconomic system ... unjust at its root'

(*EG*, no. 59), to 'an evil embedded in the structures of [a] society' (*ibid.*).

At times, it is not a question of the defence of this neo-liberal position in theory, but of the 'actual operation in the functioning of the economy' (*LS*, no. 109), of those whose 'behaviour shows that for them, maximizing profits is enough.' Yet by itself the marketplace cannot guarantee integral human development and social inclusion' (*ibid.*). These are the ends which Francis' social ethics proposes and promotes for everyone.

We need to correct the ambiguity of those who say that the Pope is condemning capitalism, if by this we mean free enterprise and the market economy. What he is rightly condemning is the ideological absolutization of the marketplace where it becomes an end rather than a means, a tool, proposed as being *self-regulated* and even as regulating all of social life without any political and ethical regulation by the state and civil society, left solely to 'unseen forces' and to its supposed 'invisible hand' (*EG*, no. 204). Consequently, despite his language being stronger and more urgent, Francis' considerations once more take up the Church's teaching on capitalism (capital work, marketplace …), especially as found in *Laborem Exercens* and *Centesimus Annus*.

In this context we understand why the Pontiff defends himself from the possible accusation of 'proposing an irresponsible populism' (*EG*, no. 204) or of wanting to offend anyone (cf. *EG*, no. 209), since he is not opposed to the marketplace nor to the science of economics, but to their becoming an ideology, in fact the dominant ideology today in practice and in theory. Today 'it is no longer simply about exploitation and oppression, but something new ... exclusion.' 'The excluded are not the "exploited" but the outcast, the "leftovers"' (*EG*, no. 53).

Francis also includes 'trickle-down' theories in his critique, which assume that economic growth encouraged by a free market will inevitably succeed in bringing about greater justice and inclusiveness in the world' (*EG*, no. 54). So, even though at times such economic growth has helped the situation of the poor in the sense that it has made them less poor, it has nevertheless generally created an even greater gap between them and the very rich and scandalously aggravated inequality which 'is the root of social ills' (*EG*, no. 202) In moral terms, this is worse than poverty itself.

Toward the end of the section I have been commenting on, the Pope draws attention to 'new forms of poverty and vulnerability, in which we are called to recognize the suffering Christ.' He lists 'the homeless, the addicted, refugees, indigenous peoples, the elderly who are increasingly isolated and abandoned' *(EG*, no. 240), 'victims of various kinds of human trafficking' (*EG*, no. 211), 'women who endure situations of exclusion, mistreatment and violence' (*EG*, no. 212), and especially 'migrants' who are forgotten (*EG*, no. 210). As we read in the daily papers, refugees and migrants are probably the majority of the victims of our time, besieged by a variety of circumstances such as wars (civil or otherwise), terrorism, urban gang violence or social exclusion, lack of a future, famine. The Pope's visit to Lampedusa soon after his election had the impact of an encyclical for many.

3.3 Cultural challenges

As described, the socio-economic system impacts on culture and vice versa, making it difficult to overcome. So, 'in the prevailing culture, priority is given to the outward, the immediate, the visible, the quick, the superficial and the provisional. What is real gives way to appearances' (*EG*, no. 62). We find ourselves amid a 'crisis of communal commitment' (from the title of *EG's* Chapter 2) in which 'the joy of living frequently fades, lack of respect for others and violence are on the rise, and inequality is increasingly evident' (*EG*, no. 208), a 'globalization of indifference' (*EG*, no. 54), 'unbridled consumerism combined with inequality' (*EG*, no. 60), and a 'throw-away culture' (cf. *EG*, no. 53).

Of course, even despite the de-christianization of much of the West, it is probably in the culture and the collective subject, civil society and religions, where we find the seeds of a better future and for overcoming the crisis. On the one hand, 'in many countries ... the Catholic Church is considered a credible institution by public opinion, and trusted for her solidarity and concern for those in greatest need' (*EG*, no. 65) and 'Christians remain steadfast in [their] intention to respect others, to heal wounds, to build bridges, to strengthen relationships and to "bear one another's burdens" (Gal 6:2)' (*EG*, no. 67). Furthermore, both within and outside the Church, Christianity and religion, 'various associations for the defence of rights and the pursuit of noble goals are being founded' and this is 'a sign of the desire of many people to contribute to social and cultural progress' (*ibid.*).

All of this gives hope, along with the emphasis placed, last of all, on the practice of mercy (Chapter 1 of this book) and the growing ecological and social concerns of many individuals and movements (which we will deal with next). These provide motives for confidence in the future, using a line from St Paul then picked up by Ricoeur in the first of his categories of hope: 'Where sin increased, grace abounded all the more.'

Chapter 2
THE SOCIALLY ACTIVE ROLE OF THE POOR AND OUTCAST

When Pope Francis spoke to the popular movements for the first time in Rome (2014) he declared that this meeting was a 'great sign' which showed 'a reality that is often silenced' brought 'into the presence of God. The poor not only suffer injustice, they also struggle against it!'[1] (*R1*).

The preferential option for the poor is also showing solidarity *with* them and implies their nature as 'active collective subjects' (*EG*, no. 122) within the Church and society. I have already said, both when speaking about the Church of the poor (for which Trigo, in the third interpretation he gives to this, supposes they are active at the practising heart of the Church) and when I referred to the 'poor Church for the poor' in Francis' words. This situates them 'at the centre of the Church's pilgrim way' (*EG*, no. 198) as an evangelizing Church, since through their popular piety they evangelize themselves in an active way (cf. *EG*, nos. 124, 126) and through 'the saving power at work in their lives' and 'the mysterious wisdom which God wishes to share with us through them' (*EG*, no. 198), they need to play an important role in the new evangelization.

---

1 FRANCIS, *Holy Father's address to participants at the World Meeting of Popular Movements, Old Synod Hall*, Tuesday 28 October 2014 (R1).

However, in this book dedicated to the Pope's social ethics, what matters more to us is the active role he assigns to the poor and to popular movements, not only in the Church but in society and for social change. He recognizes that this is part of the option for the poor in the here and now, along with interpreting reality from their position on the fringes. It is, I believe, an important and characteristic feature of the Pontiff's social ethics considered in its concrete history.

On this point, Francis' outlook extends far beyond the Catholic Church and everything we believe in Jesus, and includes all popular movements. Hence, in his first address he tells them:

> I know that you are persons of different religions, trades, ideas, cultures, countries, continents. Here and now you are practising the culture of encounter, so different from the xenophobia, discrimination and intolerance which we witness so often. Among the excluded, one finds an encounter of cultures where the aggregate does not wipe out the particularities. That is why I like the image of the polyhedron, a geometric figure with many different facets. The polyhedron reflects the confluence of all the partialities that in it keep their originality. Nothing is dissolved, nothing is destroyed, nothing is dominated, everything is integrated (*R1*, 7).

This is how the Pope imagines the worldwide network of popular movements, their interrelationship and interaction, employing themes very dear to him, like the model of the polyhedron, the culture of encounter, interculturality, even though he doesn't use this term.

1. *Kairos in the crisis situation.*

At all his encounters with the above-mentioned movements, the Pope not only expressed in each of them the profound desire for change and the perception of the urgent need for this, but also discerned the situation of the current crisis regarding them.

Later, writing to the National North American Meeting at Modesto (California, 16-19 February, 2017), he referred to the Chinese ideogram for the notion of 'crisis' to illustrate that what we are going through offers a kairos or favourable opportunity. The ideogram comprises two others, one representing danger, the other opportunity. He encouraged those he was writing to not to let this opportunity pass by.[2] Even though the risks at the ecological and social level are enormous and real, maybe even because of that we are in a favourable situation for the poor being organized into a global network of movements to make their 'historic power' felt.

2. *Actors, poets and those who make history*

Every poor, marginalized, discarded individual who is a nothing or near enough to it, can act alone for his or her own benefit, but acting together gives them strength, and more

---

[2] Cf. FRANCIS, *Holy Father's message for the Meeting of Popular Movements at Modesto*, California, 16-19 February, 2017.

so if the Spirit of the Risen Lord is motivating them, in and with them. As a result, to the question each one asks: 'What can I do?' Francis replies:

> You, the lowly, the exploited, the poor and underprivileged, can do, and are doing, a lot. I would even say that the future of humanity is in great measure in your own hands, through your ability to organize and carry out creative alternatives ... and through your proactive participation in the great processes of change on the national, regional and global levels. Don't lose heart![3]

So he not only recognizes them as active subjects but as key players both in the future and at present, in a 'great transformation.' At Santa Cruz de la Sierra (Bolivia) he would tell them:

> The future of humanity does not lie solely in the hands of the great leaders, the great powers and the elites. It is fundamentally in the hands of peoples and in their ability to organize. It is in their hands, which can guide with humility and conviction this process of change (*SCS* 11).

And here is how the Pope describes their constructive activities:

---

3 Cf. FRANCIS, 2nd World Meeting of Popular Movements. Holy Father's address, Expo Feria, Santa Cruz de la Sierra (Bolivia), Thursday 9 July 2015.

> One senses that the poor are no longer waiting. You want to be protagonists. You get organized, study, work, issue demands and above all, practise that very special solidarity that exists among those who suffer, among the poor, and that our civilization seems to have forgotten or would strongly like to forget. Solidarity … means fighting against the structural causes of poverty and inequality; of the lack of work, land and housing; and of the denial of social and labour rights. It means confronting the destructive effects of the empire of money.[4]

It is not merely a case or being prepared or of canvassing, but also and especially of acting in solidarity and non-violently against the idolizing of the god Mammon, which enslaves or discards them in structural terms. We note that here, the stress is not so much on a critique of the negative effects but on the positive aspect of the active role of movements or 'organized poor'[5] (*R2*, 4).

Hence the Pope, mentioning that 'You were inventing your own work with everything that seemed unable to give more of itself' 'with the craft skills God gave you,' tells them that 'besides work' they created 'poetry' (*R1*, 5). Then later he goes on to name 'social poets' (*R2*, 1). Further on he says

---

4 Cf. FRANCIS, Address of the Holy Father to participants at the World Meeting of Popular Movements, Old Synod Hall, Tuesday 28 October 2014.

5 Cf. FRANCIS, Holy Father's message to participants at the 3rd World Meeting of Popular Movements, Paul VI Hall, Saturday 5 November 2016 (R2).

that 'solidarity is a way of making history', as he already told them, 'that is, what popular movements do' (*R1*, 1, 2), creating history. Because it is not just about craft or art but historical change at the same time.

3. Toward authentic democracy

At his third World Meeting with Popular Movements, the Pontiff recommended they not let themselves be 'confined' to merely social action, allowing themselves to be excluded from Politics with a capital 'P', meaning non-partisan – this distinction from political parties and their ideologies is part of the specific nature of movements – but working for the *common good* (the aim of all Politics with a capital 'P'). A *new way* of engaging politically by and for civil society is being given consideration, insofar as it seeks 'universalizable' interests (Adela Cortina). These concern structural macro-relations of an economic nature or to do with power, and depend on major decisions at different levels: world, national, local. This corresponds precisely to civil society and its organizations – especially of the poor – combining both the global and the local, also macro-structures, with the culture that animates them and with the micro-relations which revitalize them.

In these times of a crisis of representation in politics this could be a path to achieving an authentic democracy, that is to say, a truly representative one because it is more participative. Without 'the active participation of peoples who seek the common good' (*R2*, 7), 'democracy atrophies, turns into a slogan, a formality, loses its representative character, and becomes disembodied, since it leaves out the people in their daily struggle for dignity, in the building of their future' (*ibid.*).

4. Tasks for constructing the common good

I will deal primarily with the content or *tasks* of the active role of popular movements, then with the *mysticism* behind it, promoting processes of radical change; and finally, how the *Church* must accompany and inspire them with its spirit (and for Christians, with its Spirit, the Spirit of Christ).

4.1 The three 'L's (in Spanish, the three 't's)

It was a recurrent theme at all three World Meetings, especially the first: *Land (tierra), Lodging (techo), Labour (trabajo)*. Francis called them 'fundamental rights' (*R1*, 1; *SCS* 1) according to the Church's social doctrine: *land* for farmers, *lodgings* and dignified *labour* for everyone as requirements which belong to their human dignity.

Land, for the Pope, means the rural community. On the one hand, it is not just their physical establishment but their existential, cultural, spiritual roots threatened not only by wars and disasters but by 'Land and water grabbing, deforestation, unsuitable pesticides' (*R1*, 2) etc.; and on the other hand, it also implies for him that there is the security of being fed because, as he puts it:

> When financial speculation manipulates the price of food, treating it as just another commodity, millions of people suffer and die from hunger. At the same time, tons of food are

thrown away. This constitutes a genuine scandal. Hunger is criminal, food is an inalienable right (*R1*, 3).

Lodging involves 'a home for every family' since 'family and housing go hand in hand' (*ibid.*); that description rules out the so-called 'street people' (*ibid.*), a euphemism which hides a blot on many of today's great cities where many of our brothers and sisters, whole families, countless children, lack a place where they can find shelter.

However, as Bergoglio had already experienced in Buenos Aires, and then picked up once more in *Laudato Si'* (cf. *LS*, no. 149), 'for a house to be a home, it requires a community dimension, and this is the neighbourhood … and it is precisely in the neighbourhood where the great family of humanity begins to be built' (*R1*, 3) which is a people. In popular neighbourhoods and settlements a rich popular culture usually flourishes and there, 'public areas are not just transit corridors but an extension of the home, a place where bonds can be forged with neighbours' (*R1*, 4). The Holy Father went on to say:

> How lovely are cities that overcome unhealthy mistrust and integrate those who are different, even making such integration a new factor of development. How lovely are cities that, in their architectural design, are full of spaces that unite, connect and foster recognition of the other. So the line to follow is neither eradication nor marginalization but urban integration (*ibid.*)

Hence, the need is not only to integrate certain districts with others and with the city as a whole and with the countryside, but, according to the Pope, to ensure that they have 'adequate infrastructure' but also 'access to health care and to education and to secure tenancy' for everyone (*ibid*).

Then *labour*: In fact, there is 'no worse material poverty than the poverty which does not allow people to earn their bread, which deprives them of the dignity of work' (ibid). Already in *Evangelii Gaudium*, Francis had linked structural unemployment, youth unemployment, informality (lack of certification) with the 'throwaway culture at work that considers humanity in itself, human beings, as a consumer good, which can be used and then thrown away' (*R1*; cf. *EG*, no. 53), because the 'deity money' has been put at the centre of the economic system, and not the human person.

In this matter of work, labour, Francis continues the legacy of earlier magisterium, especially that of St John Paul II in his Encyclical *Laborem Exercens*[6] (*LE*), where he maintains: 'It is certainly true that work, as a human issue, is at the very centre of the "social question"' (*LE*, no. 2). I would say that the novel aspect of the current Pope lies in the new context, since exclusion has been added to the exploitation of work, as a consequence of structural unemployment. It also lies in his concrete and graphic way of expressing himself, making use of strong metaphors such as *discards*, *left-overs*, *throwaway culture*, ideas already employed in the Aparecida document. Or his very concrete stories, like the

---

6   JOHN PAUL II, *Laborem Exercens*: Encyclical on human work for the 90th anniversary of *Rerum Novarum*, 14 September 1981.

Jewish Rabbi from around the year 1200. All this is then reinforced by precise statistics on youth unemployment, even though only from Europe.

4.2 Other connected problems

In these addresses, the Pope also tackles other questions of social ethics discussed at the meetings of popular movements which, according to him, cannot be simply left in the hands of political leaders. The peoples and basic communities, and hence movements made up of such are involved.

Thus the first meeting in Rome dealt with peace and taking care of nature. So, 'It is logical. There cannot be land, there cannot be housing, there cannot be work if we do not have peace and if we destroy the planet' (*R1*, 6). However, with his systematic approach, Bergoglio connects them to the very same structural causes of the serious deterioration of the three 'L's', all focused on the fetish for money, the effort to accumulate it by whatever means, including the making and sale of arms, which encourages war, or the exploitation of nature to satisfy consumerism. Everything is connected.

Other than the three 'L's', he makes reference to almost the same tasks in the meeting in Bolivia, relating them all to the urgent and profound change required today, that is: 1) put the economy at the service of peoples' (*SCS*, 6); 2) 'unite our peoples on the path of peace and justice' (*SCS*, 8), knowing how to distinguish between a healthy global interdependence and the neo-colonialism of multinationals or the monopolistic concentration of social communications media; 3) 'defend Mother Earth' (between the two meetings, Francis had published *LS*).

This repetition, and his recommendations to movements whom he considers to be protagonists of change, show that we are dealing with the very delicate themes of his social ethics which should give structure to the profound social transformation he is promoting.

Nevertheless, there is a specific and thornier concern of the Holy Father's that we need to explain for the relevance it increasingly has, entering as it does into the already mentioned problems of peace and the throwaways. I refer to 'migrants, refugees and displaced persons' (*R2*, 5). He had already taken them into serious consideration from the beginning of his pontificate, such that his first trip outside Rome was to Lampedusa, and there he spared neither words nor gestures to protect their rights and take steps to see that they are received with humanity and mercy.

It was one of the serious problems tackled at the second Rome meeting of Popular Movements (2016). In his address, Francis recognized that it was a 'world problem', the 'bankruptcy of humanity' (*R2*, 6), primarily because these people are forced to emigrate, and then because so often, when they try to do so, they fall into the hands of human traffickers, and finally, because either they are not allowed to enter a country or, not infrequently, on arriving they are looked down upon, persecuted, or exploited. In other words, they are denied basic human rights. Thus the Pope urged that:

> Some states and international agencies may open
> their eyes and take suitable measures to receive

and fully integrate all those who for one reason or another seek refuge far from home. And to confront the deeper reasons why thousands of men, women and children are daily driven from their native land (*ibid.*).

5. *The mysticism which gives energy to the process*

Francis not only gives key importance to the actors (even if they are not the only ones) involved in social transformation, but also to the spirit and mysticism of the 'processes of change'. He prioritizes 'initiating processes rather than possessing spaces' (cf. *EG*, no. 223). At Santa Cruz de la Sierra he employed very significant words to designate this mysticism: 'emotion which turns into community action.' Change begins because:

> "we have seen and heard" not a cold statistic but the pain of a suffering humanity, our own pain, our own flesh. This is something quite different than abstract theorizing or eloquent indignation. It moves us; it makes us attentive to others in an effort to move forward together (*SCS*, 4)

He is talking about *emotion*, or movement from the heart to the bowels, a visceral movement (moved, touched by the Spirit of God) but one that becomes *action*, attitude, activity, and action which is not merely personal, but essentially *communitarian*, in solidarity with many other actors, possibly coordinated in networks – even worldwide – as happens within popular movements of different character within each and between them.

This feeling of being deeply converted to a collective historic practice is, for the Pope, not something 'that can be understood by reason alone: it has a surplus of meaning which only peoples understand, and it gives a special feel to genuine popular movements' (*SCS*, 4). We note that in saying 'genuine', he is assuming that there are also false ones (later he will speak of their corruption: cf. *R2*, 8), to be precise, a criterion for discerning these will consist of this 'surplus meaning', which I have no doubt is connected with 'the affective connaturality born of love' (*EG*, no. 125) – from the Thomist tradition – and Pascal's reasons of the heart, as also with the 'more' which, as I said in the first chapter, Jon Sobrino assigns to mercy, but which here becomes creative action (like that of the craftsman or artist) which 'makes history'. I consider that the above-mentioned 'surplus meaning' adds a 'more' of historical power to the 'torrent of moral energy that springs from including the excluded in the building of a common destiny' (*R1*, 8).

However, it is about a positive process of change that we do not control, nor does the Pope, a 'great transformation' about which we know only its direction (toward the common good) and whose fruits probably others will enjoy and we will enjoy only for the anticipation of an 'already', always accompanied by a 'not yet'. Nevertheless, in his address to the third Meeting of World Popular Movements (Rome, 2016), Francis pointed to one of these anticipatory practical signs, probably motivated by the contrary treatment given refugees in both Europe and America: the fact, also visible, of pulling down *walls* and building *bridges* (cf. *R2*, 2 ff.).

The 'wall-project' comes from fear of what is other, different, foreign, what is not well known or recognized, and claims to dominate through the 'whip of fear', exercising 'basic terrorism that is born of the overall control of money worldwide and strikes at humanity as a whole' (*ibid.*, 5). But the 'bridge-project' of peoples' is opposed to 'the wall-project of money' (*ibid.*, 5) and comes, as he has already indicated, from the bowels of mercy, which is the best antidote to this fear and flows into solidarity, coordination in networks, and effective action.

This last-mentioned result is immediately connected with what I will develop in Part Three of this work concerning the Pope on discernment and the need, in order to discern properly, for 'affective conversion' from fear of what is different (wall) to love (bridge).[7]

6. *The Church's contribution*

Since Francis has discerned the historical role of the organized movement of the poor and excluded for the common good of everyone, rich and poor, Mother earth included (our common home), he has taken the decision to accompany them, but without taking their prominent role away from them. On the contrary, he urges them to join the local side of each group with the global, because:

> Real solutions to today's problems are not going to emerge from one, three or even a

---

[7] Picking up B LONERGAN's expression, 'affective conversion': cf. his article: 'Natural right and historical mindedness' in *Proceedings of the American Catholic Philosophical Association*, volume 51, 1977, Ethical Wisdom East and/or West.

> thousand conferences. They need to be the fruit
> of a collective discernment that matures on the
> ground, alongside our brothers and sisters, a
> discernment that becomes transformative action
> "in accordance with places, times and persons",
> as Saint Ignatius would say (*R2*, 2).

It is precisely Francis' focus both to reject any kind of clericalism, and to encourage 'a sound "decentralization"' (*EG*, no. 16) which Paul VI had already advised for Christian communities, and their discernment of specific situations in *Octagesimo Adveniens*. Consequently, the key concept in this context is *accompany* (without claiming to replace or direct).

Furthermore, he offers them 'a guide to action, a programme we could call revolutionary' (*R1*, 7) which he had already recommended to the youth at Rio de Janeiro: no less than the Beatitudes (according to Matthew's and Luke's Gospels) and the passage from Matthew 25 on the Last Judgement. They are radical requirements marking a spirit which not everyone will share as such. But I consider that they can serve as a leaven in the mass of movements and transform those who live them into sources of conscience for all people who in some way or other fight for justice. In other words, those moved by the spirit of the Beatitudes can be a leaven and focus even for those who fight primarily for themselves, their families and colleagues in similar situations, if it is for 'universalizable interests' (even though they coincide with their own) and for the common good.

CHAPTER 3
CARE FOR OUR COMMON HOME

1. *The current Pope's first Encyclical*

Francis has let us know that the Greek root *oikos*, which means 'home', forms part of both the word *eco*nomy and *eco*logy, so economy 'should be the art of achieving a fitting management of our common home, which is the world as a whole' (*EG*, no. 206), such that 'with due regard for the sovereignty of each nation [it] ensures the economic well-being of all countries, not just of a few' (*ibid.*) as happens at present. For its part, the ecology encourages care for our common home which is 'our sister, Mother earth' (*LS*, no. 1). Hence the close relationship between both dimensions and disciplines.

Francis' first Encyclical, as we see from its subtitle, is about 'care for our common home.' Here he combines his concern for the poor and for nature. 'The earth herself, burdened and laid waste, is among the most abandoned and maltreated of our poor; she "groans in travail" (Rom 8:22)' (*LS*, no. 2). Already in *EG*, no. 209, and in the following paragraphs referring to 'care for the vulnerable,' he said: 'There are other weak and defenceless beings who are frequently at the mercy of economic interests or indiscriminate exploitation. I am speaking of creation as a whole' (*EG*, no. 215).

The Pope describes his Encyclical as 'added to the body of the Church's social teaching' (*LS*, no. 15), addressed 'to all women and men of good will' (*LS*, no. 3) and called 'to bring the whole human family together to seek a sustainable and integral development, for we know that things can change' (*LS*, no. 13). He acknowledges 'the appeal, immensity and urgency of the challenge we face' (*LS*, no. 15). We note something typical of the Pope's tone and style of social teaching, that even faced with the most serious situations, while recognizing them as such, he loses neither 'the joy of the Gospel' and the mission to evangelize, nor does he fail to motivate everyone by showing the appeal and beauty of the urgent challenges and real possibilities for change, because for God (and for the cooperation of humankind with him and among themselves), nothing is impossible.

The Encyclical employs the method proper to the Church's social teaching: 'see, judge, act' (*MM*, no. 236). So, he begins with 'see', showing the gravity and depth of the current ecological (and social) crisis, 'drawing on the results of the best scientific research available today' (*LS*, no. 15), so we may be challenged to resolve it. He then illumines it and interprets it in the light of God's Word on creation, following this with reflection on its deepest causes ('judge'), which can be summed up in current 'technocratic' or 'techno-economic paradigms' in force, helping us to understand at greater depth what he had already described and criticized in EG, no. 53 as 'an economy that kills.' The step to 'act' is then taken with the proposal of an 'integral ecology' and 'lines of approach and action' focused on dialogue at all levels. Finally, faithful to himself and his appreciation of the cultural change needed for structural change, Bergoglio places his emphasis on a new motivating spirituality, a new lifestyle, and new educational change to achieve it (cf. *LS*, no. 5).

The introduction to the Encyclical not only presents us with a development of his thinking in its various chapters, but also alerts us to 'a number of themes which will reappear as the Encyclical unfolds' (*LS*, no. 16), themes which 'will not be dealt with once and for all, but re-framed and enriched again and again' (*ibid.*) in each new section. As examples he says he will point to:

> the intimate relationship between the poor and the fragility of the planet, the conviction that everything in the world is connected, the critique of new paradigms and forms of power derived from technology, the call to seek other ways of understanding the economy and progress, the value proper to each creature, the human meaning of ecology, the need for forthright and honest debate, the serious responsibility of international and local policy, the throwaway culture and the proposal of a new lifestyle (*LS*, no. 16).

Each phrase in this paragraph is replete with content, and as a whole it sums up the new contribution Francis makes to the wealth of the Church's thinking on social issues.

The paragraph also confirms two assertions by Carlos Leyva on the Encyclical[1] with which I am in complete agreement: 1) that it deals with the challenge it is tackling by thinking it through *systematically*, and 2) that it does so from the perspective of the periphery, not the centre, meaning from where people who suffer most from the crisis are: the poor and excluded, including the earth and all living beings believing in life, especially human life.

2. See' 'what is happening to our common home' (LS, no. 17 ff.)

Pollution, climate change, energy sources that are neither clean nor renewable, the poor quality and scarcity of water, loss of biodiversity, disturbance to ecosystems, accumulation of waste and toxic substances, the 'throwaway culture', etc., etc., are factors which affect the way we inhabit the earth, its viability for a dignified life and the universal exploitation of common goods such as climate, clean air or drinkable water. Everyone suffers in some way, but especially the billions of poor people, in other words the majority of humankind today. Hence:

> Human beings too are creatures of this world, enjoying a right to life and happiness, and endowed with unique dignity. So we cannot fail to consider the effects on people's lives of environmental deterioration, current models of development and the throwaway culture (*LS*, no. 43),

---

1 Cf. C Leyva, *Economía y política según* Laudato Si', in the commentary on the Encyclical by the Farrel Group CICCUS, Buenos Aires, 2017.

especially for people on the margins, like the excluded and discarded who are in the majority.

Nevertheless, even though there is shared responsibility here, it is 'differentiated' (*LS*, no. 53) since the rich North has an 'ecological debt' (*LS*, no. 51) regarding the poor South, resulting in a 'global inequality' at an international level (*LS*, no. 48).

Further on, when the Holy Father 'judges' the situation described in the first chapter of *LS*, and it is illuminated by the Word of God (in the second chapter) with a view to how to 'act', he says that nature is not 'something separate from ourselves' or 'a mere setting in which we live. We are part of nature, included in it and thus in constant interaction with it' (*LS*, no. 139). Everything is interrelated: nature, institutions, customs, culture. Hence 'recognizing the reasons why a given area is polluted requires a study of the workings of society, its economy, its behaviour patterns, and the way it grasps reality' (*ibid.*), because there are 'not two separate crises, one environmental and the other social, but rather one complex crisis which is both social and environmental' (*ibid.*). *LS*, when it refers to ecological degradation, almost always then goes on to consider the social impact and vice versa. I consider that this appreciation of a single crisis is one of the most important ones in the Encyclical, articulated through his interpretation of its deepest foundation and his proposal for a solution which points to unity in complexity.

Further on in the same Encyclical he attempts to get to the ultimate root of the crisis in the human setting, namely, the *sociocultural paradigm* currently in vogue, which is the *same* both for our relationship with nature and with other people, especially the weakest among them. This is the technocratic paradigm. He goes on to promote a response to this crisis: *integral* ecology. These are all key concepts for understanding Francis' social ethics, derived from his interpretation of 'what is happening to our common home' and to those living in it, especially to the most defenceless.

3. *Theology of creation*

It is not only the sciences – which the Pope gave much consideration to in the first chapter of the Encyclical – that must contribute to the resolution of this deep crisis, but also the cultural wisdom of the peoples and their religions, so important for motivating the necessary changes, according to philosophers like Jügen Habermas for what he calls our post-secular era. In this point too, we note the importance of culture and cultures in Francis' view of reality and its transformation.

In the second chapter of his Encyclical, he presents the contribution biblical faith makes to a wisdom-based understanding of the ecological problem which allows him to link 'the Gospel of creation' which he presents there, with the mention above of the essential priority of mercy. Scripture conceives of creation as a prime gift prior to human freedom which modernity places at the centre.

Even though faith recognizes the 'infinite dignity' of each human person who is 'not just something but someone' (*LS*, no. 65), just the same it also accepts 'a mutual responsibility between human beings and nature' (*LS*, no. 67), as also 'responsibility for God's earth' (*LS*, no. 68) and hence there can never be a claim to 'absolute ownership' by anyone (*LS*, no. 67).

So it is, while affirming the 'immense dignity' of human beings, that the Bible also teaches that 'each creature possesses its own particular goodness and perfection' (*LS*, no. 69) and that 'other living beings have a value of their own in God's eyes' (*ibid.*) – since they possess 'inherent laws' which human beings must respect, and which, therefore, means we can speak of 'the priority of being over that of being useful' (*ibid.*).

> 'Everything is interconnected' (*LS*, no. 70) so that 'as part of the universe, called into being by one Father, all of us are linked by unseen bonds and together form a kind of universal family, a sublime communion which fills us with a sacred, affectionate and humble respect' (*LS*, no. 89).

It is clear that communion respects differences, according tot he model of the polyhedron, for which

> It is clearly inconsistent to combat trafficking in endangered species while remaining indifferent to human trafficking, unconcerned about the poor, or undertaking to destroy another human being deemed unwanted (*LS*, no. 91).

4. *The common destination of goods*

Consistent with his view that there is but one crisis which is social and environmental together, Francis reiterates that 'every ecological approach needs to incorporate a social perspective which takes into account the fundamental rights of the poor and the underprivileged' (*LS*, no. 93), since 'the earth is essentially a shred inheritance whose fruits are meant to benefit everyone' (*ibid*.). Believers and non-believers today are in agreement with this.

In this context, the Pope quotes the Encyclical *Laborem Exercens*, no. 19, where St John Paul II states that ' the principle of the subordination of private property to the universal destination of goods' is 'the first principle of the whole ethical and social order' (*LS*, no. 93).

However, he does so by employing the formula frequently used in the Church's social teaching, 'universal destination of goods', and by adopting the same focus as in *EG*, no. 189 which emphasizes its priority over private property. For himself and John Paul private property is seen not as absolute but as having a social mortgage. Consequently, the current Pope adds a practical conclusion of this 'first principle', namely, that 'the right of everyone to their use ['of goods'] is a golden rule of social conduct' (*ibid*.).

It follows that every action which hinders or gets in the way of this common destination, excluding others, people and/or peoples from this destination, contradicts 'the first principle of the whole social and ethical order.' Hence we are dealing with another key *elements* of the Holy Father Francis' social ethics, consistent with the Church's traditional teaching which today, faced with this crisis, is more appropriate than ever to recall and encourage.

However, 'this right must be guaranteed so that its exercise is not illusory but real' (*LS*, no. 94). By way of example the Pope then cites the bishops of Paraguay when they refer to the 'natural right' of every *campesino* to have 'a reasonable allotment of land.' They add: 'apart from the ownership of property, rural people must have access to means of technical education, credit, insurance and markets' (*ibid.*). In each case, not only is there need to claim the right in abstract but also to contribute to fulfilling the conditions for them to be effective in fact, and so that the goods of this world – including collective goods such as the natural environment (*LS*, no. 95) – are recognized as ' the patrimony of all humanity and the responsibility of everyone' (*ibid.*), created and destined for all.

5. *The technocratic paradigm*

As is known, Bergoglio was thinking of writing his doctoral thesis on the theology of Romano Guardini. So it is no surprise that he cites this author in his Encyclical, from his work *The End of the Modern World*, convinced as he is that we are experiencing an historic change and are going through a crisis caused by modernity's sociocultural paradigm. Bergoglio calls it 'technocratic' (*LS*, no. 106) and 'techno-economic' (*LS*, no. 203) and describes it as 'undifferentiated and one-dimensional' (*LS*, no. 106). What predominates is:

> the tendency, at times unconscious, to make the method and aims of science and technology an epistemological paradigm which shapes the lives of individuals and the working of society (*LS*, no. 107).

It includes the economy and politics (cf. *LS*, no. 109), all 'situations conditioned by technology, itself viewed as the principle key to the meaning of existence' (*LS*, no. 110). Neither technoscience nor technology are criticized in themselves, but their extrapolation as a cultural horizon for understanding life as a whole, our co-existence among ourselves and with nature, 'which leads to the planet being squeezed dry beyond every limit' (*LS*, no. 106) in the endeavour 'to extract everything possible from [it]' (*ibid.*).

We recall that in Germany during Guardini's time, Martin Heidegger was already warning against *Gestell* or technology understood as guiding the destiny of being. The first Frankfurt School (Theodor Adorno, Max Horkheimer) produced a philosophical critique of the absolutization of instrumental reason. Yet it is not a matter of rejecting technology but one of not making it the ultimate measure of everything, the ultimate cultural horizon 'as if the subject were to find itself in the presence of something formless, completely open to manipulation' (*LS*, no. 106). On the contrary, of itself 'technoscience, when well directed, can produce important means of improving the quality of human life.' It can 'also produce art and enable men and women … to "leap" into the world of beauty' (*LS*, no. 103).

Not even Guardini's reflections on power cease to influence Bergoglio; in this case the tremendous power technology offers today, not only to human beings in general but to 'those with the knowledge, and especially the economic power to use [it],' giving them 'an impressive dominance over the whole of humanity and the entire world' (*LS*, no. 104). Hence the risk that such power 'lies with a small part of humanity' (*ibid.*) because we have the painful experience that 'freedom fades when it is handed over to the blind forces of the unconscious, of immediate needs, of self-interest, and of violence ... exposed in the face of our ever-increasing power, lacking the wherewithal to control it' (*LS*, no. 105).

Thus the Pope calls for 'a sound ethics, a culture and spirituality' (*ibid.*) which presume a solid anthropology. We note that the Holy Father appeals to the theme of culture and combines it with that of spirituality, which he will pick up again later. They are essential components of his sound social ethics.

Kant's u-turn from things in their reality to the autonomous subject who proposes and disposes of them *a priori*, is not only typical of modern philosophy but symbolizes modernity in its cultural totality. Also the Heideggerian inflection represents 'the end of the modern era' in general and not only of its philosophy, since, as Ricoeur says, by now we no longer conceive of thought as imposed on being, and thus reducing reality of things and people in themselves to mere objects of a subject but, on the contrary, we recognize that being gives itself to thought as an original gift which calls on one to think. At the philosophical level it is enough to cite the ethics of difference of Emmanuel Levinas and the phenomenology of gift of Jean-Luc Marion, and at the level of Christian social doctrine, Benedict XVI's Encyclical *Caritas in Veritate*, with its emphasis on the gift economy developed through the logic of the marketplace and the state, which it informs and transforms.

Francis is already moving within this new cultural setting – more suited to the gospel – and, in practice, advances in the same direction not only because he applies this reasoning of 'new thinking' to social and environmental ecology, but also because he sums up what has to be overcome, and the approaches of a new cultural logic through the rich category of the 'paradigm'. As I interpret it, such a monumental change corresponds not only to 'the end of the modern era', but to the new assessment of gift, diversity, communion and the interrelationships in contemporary thought, which at the same time is planting the seed of new and emerging practices both in the ecological and social setting, which *LS* points to as reactions of authentic humanity to the technocratic paradigm. See the examples of 'authentic rising up in resistance' which Francis lists in *LS*, no. 112 among others. He brings them together in a beautiful metaphor, saying

> An authentic humanity, calling for a new synthesis, seems to dwell in the midst of our technological culture, almost unnoticed, like a mist seeping gently beneath a closed door (*ibid.*).

Francis does not explicitly describe this 'new synthesis' (*ibid.*, cf. Also *LS*, no. 121) which authentic humanity is inviting us to, a 'new paradigm', but presents it matter of factly in its main desirable features when he describes the ecological culture:

> There needs to be a distinctive way of looking at things, a way of thinking, policies, an educational

> programme, a lifestyle and a spirituality which together generate resistance to the assault of the technocratic paradigm (*LS*, no. 111).

In my opinion, we are dealing here not only with mere resistance, but also an incipient creativity (to which the Pontiff himself will allude in the following chapters of his Encyclical).

In 2006, the Faculties of Philosophy and Theology at San Miguel (where Bergoglio studied, graduated, then later became its Vice Chancellor and Rector) organized an interdisciplinary Congress on the question: 'Communion: a new paradigm?'[2] Toward the end of this event, German theologian, Peter Hünermann, drew up a kind of conclusion saying that while it may not be providing a change of cultural paradigm, it is at least certain that what is taking place in culture and in the disciplines mentioned was a change of emphasis and language. I consider that Francis, with his charism of discernment, has not failed to perceive this.

Hence we need to conclude with him that we cannot

> disregard any aspect of reality: 'Peace, justice and the preservation of creation are three absolutely interconnected themes, which cannot be separated and treated individually without falling into reductionism' (*LS*, no. 92, quoting the Dominican Bishops Conference).

---

2 Cf. JL MARION (et al): *Comunión: ¿un nuevo paradigma? Congreso internacional de Teología, Filosofía y Ciencias Sociales*, San Benito, Buenos Aires, 2006.

In order to tackle these, we need 'to move forward in a bold cultural revolution' (*LS*, no. 114). This presumes we can discern 'unrestrained delusions of grandeur' from the 'positive and sustainable progress' of science and modern technology. Thus the third part of this work will tackle the problem of discernment as a fundamental element – of method, not just content – of Francis' theological and social ethics.

6. *Ecology and anthropology*

Since 'everything is interrelated' (*LS*, no. 120; cf. no. 117), 'there can be no ecology without an adequate anthropology' (*LS*, no. 118), since the relationship of the human being with nature depends on the idea we have of it. Hence his Christian understanding of 'responsible stewardship' (*LS*, no. 116) contrasts with an 'excessive anthropocentrism' (*ibid.*) which is our 'modern anthropocentrism' (*LS*, no. 115). This ends up as today's 'practical relativism' (*LS*, no. 122) whose logic, focused on its own immediate interests, has led to the serious consequences which the Pope indicates in *LS*, no. 123. Faithful to his assessment of the important role of culture in societies, the Holy Father observes that then, 'culture itself is corrupt' (*ibid.*). In Lonergan's terminology, this leads to 'social absurdity'.

But if the human person is conceived of as a 'responsible steward' of nature, caring for it and creatively transforming it, but responsibly, 'to bring out the potential which [God] himself inscribed in things' (*LS*, no. 124), an 'adequate anthropology' implies 'taking account of the value of labour, as Saint John Paul II wisely noted in his Encyclical *Laborem Exercens'* (*ibid.*). Like his predecessors, Francis refers not only to manual work, but to any 'activity involving a modification of existing reality, from producing a social report to the design of a technological development' (*LS*, no. 125). So, 'work is a necessity, part of the meaning of life on this earth, a path to growth, human development and personal fulfilment' (*LS*, no. 128).

It follows that 'in the reality of today's global society it is essential that' (and here he quotes *Caritas in Veritate*, no. 32) "we continue to prioritize the goal of access to steady employment for everyone," no matter the limited interests of business and dubious economic reasoning' (*LS*, no. 127). Hence the Holy Father, while praising 'business' as 'a noble vocation, directed to producing wealth and improving our world,' reminds it that 'the creation of jobs [is] an essential part of its service to the common good' (*LS*, no. 129).

In no way does the Pontiff want to restrict scientific creativity and technology, even in the search for new forms of human work for those replaced by machines, but, in defence of 'our Sister, Mother Earth' and the poor and excluded, he wants to disconnect creativity from economic, political and ideological interests so it is at the service of the common good and the universal destination of the goods of creation.

7. *Toward an integral ecology*

I regard it as no coincidence that the Pope has introduced – for the first time in *LS* – the key concept of 'integral ecology', which he picks up again when turning to Francis of Assisi as 'an attractive and compelling figure' whose 'name [he] took as [his] guide and inspiration when [he] was elected Bishop of Rome' (*LS*, no. 10). Furthermore, the beginning of the *Canticle of the Creatures* by the Saint of Assisi gave him the title of his Encyclical. The adjective 'integral' not only reminds us of what the crisis is, because it is both social and environmental, but indicates the next steps to be taken in Chapter Four of *LS*, beginning with a section on 'environmental, economic and social ecology' (which responds more directly to the description given of a single crisis), to then refer to the 'cultural ecology' which sustains it and, finally, moving to the 'ecology of daily life', extending it to the most concrete aspects of everyday, without losing its inclusive nature as an overall response to the technocratic paradigm.

This integral way of looking at things must take account of all the factors, 'since everything is closely interrelated' (*LS*, no. 137; cf. no. 138, etc.) and the crisis is one, although a complex one. As a result, 'it is essential to seek comprehensive solutions which consider the interaction within natural systems themselves and with social systems' (*LS*, no. 139). When we speak of the environment and ecology, 'what we really mean is a relationship existing between nature and the society which lives in it' (*ibid.*). So before dealing with the crisis, it is necessary to reflect on and debate 'the conditions required for the life and survival of society' which have produced it and are aggravating it, with the 'honesty needed to question certain *models of development, production and consumption*' (*LS*, no. 138; italics mine). They are not only economic but also social and cultural.

Such reflection and free debate and the corresponding interdisciplinary investigation must not only bear in mind the relationship between nature and society (its value of 'sustainable use' and also rational use) but also the 'intrinsic value independent of their usefulness' (*LS*, no. 140) of each organism and ecosystem. 'Each organism, as a creature of God, is good and admirable in itself' (*ibid.*). In order to act justly for the coming generations, 'consideration must always be given to each ecosystem's regenerative ability, in its different areas and aspects' (*ibid.*).

The Holy Father immediately shows how a truly integral ecology is also an economic one, not merely an environmental one (cf. LS, no. 141) - and a social one (LS, no. 142) at the same time, which 'is necessarily institutional, and gradually extends to the whole of society from the primary social group, the family, to the wider local, national and international communities' (*ibid.*).

The Encyclical then dedicates a special section to cultural ecology, given the significance Francis gives to culture and cultures 'which cannot be excluded as we rethink the relationship between human beings and the environment' (*LS*, no. 143).

Then, just as he deals with the preservation of plant and animal species, we should be even more concerned with the preservation of cultures, their valuable diversity and cultural riches (cf. *LS*, no. 145), in fruitful dialogue between scientific-technical language and the wisdom and language of the people. Today there is 'an historic, artistic and cultural patrimony' which is 'likewise under threat' (*LS*, no. 143).

Hence the need to respect the rights of peoples and cultures and reject any levelling of cultures, consumerism and a cultural feature and uniform ecological solutions or merely technical ones (cf. *LS*, no. 144) which do not take sufficient account of the local cultural perspective, especially of indigenous communities (cf. *LS*, no. 146).

8. *The common good*

After having dealt with the human and environmental ecology in a holistic way, and after having shown that it is the one, although complex, issue, the Pope goes to the root of the matter by saying: 'Human ecology is inseparable from the notion of the common good' (*LS*, no. 156). This is also characterized by its integral nature such that it extends even to the environment as one common good. We note the importance he gives to this, observing that it is 'a central and unifying principle of social ethics' (*LS*, no. 156) in general and, of course, also in the particular focus he is adopting. In order to formulate it he uses the words of *Gaudium et Spes*, no. 26, namely: 'the sum of those conditions of social life which allow social groups and their individual members relatively thorough and ready access to their own fulfillment' (*LS*, no. 156). This does not list content but speaks of 'conditions' and 'possibilities', extending them to everyone in such a way that it can adapt according to the variety of historical eras and cultural spaces while at the same time reaffirming its essential universality.

The Holy Father then immediately relates it to the Church's doctrine and social ethics, connecting it with its foundation, which is the dignity and 'respect for the human person as such, endowed with basic and inalienable rights' and its purpose, adding that they are 'ordered to his or her integral development' (*LS*, no. 157). In alluding to the 'overall welfare of society and the development of a variety of intermediate groups' he explains the principle of subsidiarity, since 'outstanding among these groups is the family, as the basic cell of all of society' (*ibid.*), but also, in saying that 'the common good calls for social peace, the stability and security provided by a certain order which cannot be achieved without particular concern for distributive justice,' he is also referring to the other complementary principle, that of solidarity, hence both solidarity and subsidiarity flow immediately from the central principle of the common good, which in turn is based on human dignity and social interaction. Last of all, as a culmination of this paragraph, Francis reminds us of who should protect it: 'Society as a whole, and the state in particular, are obliged to defend and promote the common good' (*ibid.*). In just one paragraph he offers us a small treatise on this core theme of Christian social doctrine in general, and of the Encyclical in particular.

Francis does not remain just at the theoretical level of doctrine, but in the following paragraph, situates it within 'the present condition of global society, where injustices abound and growing numbers of people are deprived of basic human rights and considered expendable' (*LS*, no. 158). Here and now, in this era of globalization and exclusion, 'the principle of the common good immediately becomes ... a summons to solidarity and a preferential option for the poorest of our brothers and sisters' (*ibid.*).

Just as the *Compendium of the Church's Social Doctrine* deals with the universal use of goods as an application of the principle of the common good, the Pope too, urged on by the serious situation and crisis we are going through, adds: 'This opinion entails recognizing the implications of the universal destination of the immense dignity of the poor' (*ibid.*). He adds: 'We need only look around us to see that, today, this option is in fact an ethical imperative essential for effectively attaining the common good.' So, to 'seeing', corresponds both this 'judging' and 'acting' with its radical consequences.

But the adjective 'common' in 'the notion of the common good also extends to future generations' (*LS*, no. 159) and an 'inter-generational solidarity' as a 'basic question of justice' (*ibid.*). However, it is not only about the environment, but an *integral* ecology, meaning 'when we ask ourselves what kind of world we want to leave behind, we think in the first place of its general direction, its meaning and its values' (*LS*, no. 160).

And thus it is, in these individualist post-modern times when we want everything now, that the question is posed of the meaning of life and living with one another and with our Sister, Mother Earth, in intra- and inter-generational solidarity. Once again we see the significance that the cultural dimension has for him, the core of which is the ultimate meaning of life.

9. *Dialogue for a culture of encounter*

9.1 At the international level

The fifth chapter of the Encyclical tackles 'some lines of approach and action' which correspond to the previous 'seeing' how things are now, and 'judging' which are both the root of the human crisis – the technocratic paradigm – and the summary expression of a solution: an integral ecology. If we note the subtitles of the various sections of the chapter, we will see that they all include the word 'dialogue', corresponding to the other of Bergoglio's *leitmotifs*: *'the culture of encounter'*.

Above all, dialogue needs to happen at various levels, given that we still lack 'stronger and more efficiently organized international institutions, with functionaries who are appointed fairly by agreement among national governments, and empowered to impose sanctions' (*LS*, no. 175), in other words, 'a true world political authority' (*ibid.*), as proposed by Benedict XVI and already indicated by John XXIII. In the meantime, until this is achieved, 'diplomacy takes on new importance in the work of developing international strategies which can anticipate serious problems affecting us all' (*ibid.*).

This now makes international political dialogue essential in 'an interdependent world' which 'obliges us to think of one world with a common plan' (*LS*, no. 164) for we who are living in our common home. It is not only a matter of avoiding environmental damage and global social problems, but more importantly, of finding 'solutions that are proposed from a global perspective, and not simply to defend the interests of a few countries' (*LS*, no. 164). Here too, the priority of the common good, of the whole over the part, is valid.

Thought needs to be given to who will shoulder the costs of adopting such solutions – for example, the drastic change in energy sources from 'highly polluting fossil fuels – especially coal, but also oil and, to a lesser degree, gas' (*LS*, no. 165) to clean and renewable energy. So, 'there is a need for common and differentiated responsibilities' (*LS*, no. 170). It is unjust that 'countries which have experienced great growth at the cost of ongoing pollution of the planet' (*LS*, no. 172) and/or 'have benefited from a high degree of industrialization, at the cost of enormous emissions of greenhouse gases' (*LS*, no. 170) are on par with countries in need of development, and thus have fewer resources. They need help in order to access technology transfer.

The need for 'enforceable international agreements' and corresponding 'global regulatory norms' is not only 'to prevent unacceptable actions, for example, when powerful companies dump contaminated waste or offshore polluting industries in other countries' (*LS*, no. 173), but also to ensure 'governance for the whole range of so-called "global commons"' (*LS*, no. 174), for example, 'marine waste and the protection of the open seas' (*ibid.*).

The worldwide ecological movement and the various international summits on the environment, especially the Earth Summit (Rio de Janeiro, 1992), 'have given rise to considerable public debate and have elicited a variety of committed and generous civic responses' (*LS*, no. 165), encouraging greater cultural ecological awareness and effective transformations. Yet 'politics and business have been slow to react in a way commensurate with the urgency of the challenges facing the world' (*ibid.*). Hence the need for greater pressure to be put on them for civil society to achieve real consensus.

9.2 National and local levels

Differentiated responsibility applies not only at the international level but also at lower levels, even within poor countries which also have their 'winners and losers' (*LS*, no. 176). Hence 'individual states can no longer ignore their responsibility for planning, coordination, oversight and enforcement within their respective borders' (*LS*, no. 177), so that not only is poor practice avoided, but they 'stimulate creativity in seeking new solutions' through 'individual or group initiatives' (*ibid.*).

Not infrequently, politicians prefer holding onto positions of power rather than initiating processes of renewal over time which would bring medium- or long-term benefits. Civil society, though, considers the medium- and long-term possibilities, and in many places 'cooperatives are being developed to exploit renewable sources of energy,' showing that 'local individuals and groups can make a difference'

(*LS*, no. 179). Experience and daily practice also teach that:

> because the enforcement of laws is at times inadequate due to corruption, public pressure has to be exerted in order to bring about decisive political action. Society, through non-governmental organizations and political groups, must put pressure on governments to develop more rigorous regulations, procedures and controls' (*ibid.*).

This contradicts 'the mindset of short-term gain and results which dominates present-day economics and politics' (*LS*, no. 181). Therefore, without ignoring other levels, so much can be done at local and municipal level, thanks to the initiative and pressure of living forces among the people. They are the ones, after all, who suffer the most immediate consequences of environmental and social degradation.

It follows from this that decision-making processes should be marked by open dialogue and transparency, free of hidden motives and corruption. I do not intend here to summarize the healthy criteria for taking these kinds of decisions which the Holy Father develops in nos. 182–187 of his Encyclical, but just indicate that they are all guided by the common good, from which one can draw, among other things, interdisciplinary collaboration, communication without holding back pertinent information, active involvement by all affected parties, especially local inhabitants, etc.

The Pope concludes this section by reminding people 'that the Church does not presume to settle scientific questions or to replace politics' but invites them 'to encourage an honest and open debate so that particular interests or ideologies will not prejudice the common good' (*LS*, no. 188). As we observe, this idea is central for Francis.

9.3 Politics and economy in dialogue for human fulfilment

We get the feeling that at this stage of his consideration of 'some lines of approach and action,' before taking a further step in the following chapter, the Pontiff has felt the need to summarize his thinking on social ethics once more. This time, however, by contrast with how he did so previously, he places the emphasis on positive proposals, without forgetting the negative signs, but contrasting the two, preparing for what he will be proposing in the final chapter of the Encyclical.

He reaffirms that 'politics should not be subject to the economy, nor should the economy be subject to the dictates of an efficiency-driven paradigm of technocracy' (*LS*, no. 189). We need both 'to enter into a frank dialogue in the service of life, especially human life' (*ibid*).

Just the same, in this new attempt at synthesis, the Pope again criticizes 'the principle of the maximization of profits, frequently isolated from other considerations' (*LS*, no. 195), 'an instrumental way of reasoning ... at work whether resources are allocated by the market or by state central planning' (*ibid*.) and similarly, the current 'absolute power of a financial system' which, during the 2007–2008 crisis, reasserted itself by 'saving banks at any cost, making the public pay the price, forgoing a firm commitment to reviewing and reforming the entire system' and without 'new ways of regulating speculative financial practices and virtual wealth' (*LS*, no. 189). Indirectly, he is urging review and reform of the entire system through a healthy regulation of the financial system.

In opposition to these negative experiences, the Pope proposes a creative search, involving dialogue for 'new models of progress' (*LS*, no. 194) and for 'sustainable and equitable development within the context of a broader concept of quality of life' (*LS* no. 192). 'It is not enough to include a few superficial ecological considerations while failing to question the logic which underlies present-day culture' (*LS*, no. 197). This is precisely what Francis does in and through his Encyclical, in agreement with a new way of thinking based on the common good and common goods, including the environment, mother earth, and climate.

9.4 Dialogue between religions and science

An effective response to the social and ecological crisis requires a change in a cultural way of thinking. For this, as the final step of the fourth chapter of *LS*, the Holy Father goes back to the need for dialogue between religions and science. Along with the serious and impartial study the sciences need to offer by working in an interdisciplinary manner, we need to add the *ethical motivation* which religions alone can offer. This has recently been recognized by philosophers like Habermas.[3]

---

3 Amongst the various works, cf. J HABERMAS, *Between naturalism and religion*. Translated by Ciaran Cronin. Polity Press,

The crisis is so great that dialogue between sciences and among religions themselves has become urgent, along with dialogue between religious wisdom and science. The reality is that:

> The majority of people living on our planet profess to be believers. This should spur religions to dialogue among themselves for the sake of protecting nature, defending the poor, and building networks of respect and fraternity (*LS*, no. 201).

So, concluding, only honest and sincere dialogue, the search for and achievement of consensus on basic points, and putting these into practice for the common good, with due controls and possible sanctions, can save us from the likely social and environmental catastrophes which the mere logic of the technocratic paradigm is leading us to.

9.5 Spirituality, education and ecological conversion

9.5.1 Change of lifestyle

Everything the Encyclical has said thus far leads us to the fact that 'a great cultural, spiritual and educational challenge stands before us, and it will demand that we set out on the long path of renewal' (*LS*, no. 202) since today 'we lack an awareness of our common origin, of our mutual belonging, and of a future to be shared with everyone' (*ibid.*). Opposed to this is 'compulsive consumerism' which reflects the 'techno-

Cambridge, UK, 2008,

economic paradigm' which reduces freedom to 'the supposed freedom to consume. But those really free are the minority who wield economic and financial power' (*ibid.*).

Hence the need for a cultural change or, in other words, change of 'lifestyle' and of our individualist and consumerist way of thinking to an 'alternative,' unselfish one. It is possible for people 'despite their mental and social conditioning' (*LS*, no. 205). We human beings 'are able to take an honest look at ourselves, to acknowledge our deep dissatisfaction, and to embark on new paths to authentic freedom' (*ibid.*). The Pope has been giving examples of individuals, organizations and movements throughout the Encyclical, and I have noted them in my text. 'No system can completely suppress our openness to what is good, true and beautiful, or our God-given ability to respond to his grace at work deep in our hearts' (*ibid.*). 'We are always capable of going out of ourselves towards the other' (*LS*, no. 208), toward others, the other, every other. Here lies the real possibility for change, as it is in fact already occurring in many people.

Furthermore, such transformations of lifestyle in society can 'bring healthy pressure to bear on those who wield political, economic and social power' (*LS*, no. 206), as has happened with certain businesses thanks to consumer movements. We recall that after the class struggle during the second half of the 19th century and the first half of the 20th century, the *alliance* of union movements (those pushing from below) *with* those from above who were *intelligently* seeking their interests (so as not to reduce them significantly because of strikes, or not to lose everything due to a communist takeover of power), made possible for Rhine countries the *social* market economy and the *social welfare* State which aims at an equitable approach to the most neglected. Globalization has put much of what was achieved at risk, but a similar alliance at global level should not be excluded.

9.5.2 The importance of education

To achieve such cultural change, which in turn conditions the necessary structural changes, it is essential for education to change. Therefore, 'an awareness of the gravity of today's cultural and ecological crisis must be translated into new habits' (*LS*, no. 209) which will be achieved through education. A key opportunity is offered by the fact that 'in those countries which should be making the greatest changes in consumer habits, young people have a new ecological sensitivity and a generous spirit' (*ibid.*) even though 'they have grown up in a milieu of extreme consumerism and affluence which makes it difficult to develop other habits' (*ibid.*). This is the 'educational challenge'.

In response to this, the first educator is the family, followed by the school – the primary school above all – but the whole of society, the State and the Church, have an important role to play as well (cf. *LS*, no. 213. 214).

It is not just about giving out information of a social and ecological kind, as scientific as it may be, but of encouraging new habits in behaviour, based on theoretical premises but especially solid practical reasons that appeal to the heart. Francis observes that:

> It needs educators capable of developing an ethics of ecology, and helping people, through effective pedagogy, to grow in solidarity, responsibility and compassionate care (*LS*, no. 210).

We recall, in this context, everything said above about tenderness and mercy, to which the Pope adds 'a good aesthetic education, because 'by learning to see and appreciate beauty, we learn to reject self-interested pragmatism' (*LS*, no. 215). There is a need to touch the sensitive side and the heart of individuals and peoples because, in the end, it is about achieving a true conversion.

9.5.3 Toward an ecological conversion

Francis then specifically addresses Christians, reminding them of their ecological spirituality, 'the fruit of twenty centuries of personal and communal experience' (*LS*, no. 216), one of whose principal models is his patron, St Francis of Assisi (cf. *LS*, no. 218). 'More than in ideas and concepts as such, I am interested in how such a spirituality can motivate us to a more passionate concern for the protection of our world.' He is interested in a 'spirituality capable of inspiring us,' 'an interior impulse which encourages, motivates, nourishes and gives meaning to our individual and communal activity (*EG*, no. 216)' (*LS*, no. 216). Models are more effective for this than doctrines. Especially because today what is needed is an 'ecological conversion' (*LS*, no. 217) also for believers, since 'living our vocation to be protectors of God's handiwork is essential to a life of virtue; it is not an optional or a secondary aspect of our Christian experience' (*ibid.*).

Nevertheless, the conversion of isolated individuals is not enough to overcome the logic of instrumental reason, today absolutized and become a cultural paradigm. 'The ecological conversion needed to bring about lasting change is also a community conversion' (*LS*, no. 219). Faced with enormous environmental and human degradation, this kind of conversion has been growing in the different ecological movements, and among 'green' politicians, in the cultivation of disciplines such as eco-philosophy and eco-theology, and is promoted now not only in the great community of the Catholic Church by its universal Pastor, but is also addressed to all women and men of good will.

Then the Holy Father goes on to describe attitudes which this conversion presumes as a basis for the new habits, lifestyles and culture. He highlights among these: 'generous care, full of tenderness,' 'self-sacrifice and good works,' 'a loving awareness that we are not disconnected from the rest of creatures, but joined in a splendid universal communion (*LS*, no. 220).

9.6 The fruits of Christian spirituality and its trinitarian foundation

In close relationship with what was presented earlier in the second chapter on the gospel of creation, the Pontiff shows some of its fruits, made concrete and brought about by the integral ecological conversion he has just spoken of, as also by the new spirituality which it leads to and which springs from it. The subtitles of the sections of *LS* to follow, point to these fruits, which partly coincide with the 'fruits of the Holy Spirit' which theology speaks of – such as joy, peace and love which are personal, social and political. These flourish to the extent that integral ecological conversion is realized in cultures, overcoming the dominance of the technocratic paradigm. It assumes 'sobriety and humility' which 'were not favourably regarded in the last century' (*LS*, no. 224).

Already at the beginning of the Encyclical, Francis poses the axiom 'everything is connected' (*LS*, no. 16) as one of the guidelines that *LS* 'takes up and re-examines' (*ibid.*) time and time again, and we see this in practically every chapter. Now at the end, in the context of the contributions of the Christian faith and spirituality, the trinitarian foundation of this key expression is clearly described in its vivid nature for Bergoglio. The Trinity is the foundation of the spirit of the entire Encyclical and even of his entire social ethics. As he puts it: 'everything is interconnected, and this invites us to develop a spirituality of that global solidarity which flows from the mystery of the Trinity' (*LS*, no. 240).

Earlier, I indicated two grounds and aspects of these trinitarian roots, one in reference to the Trinity in itself, and the other to its imprint on creation. He says: 'The divine Persons are subsistent relations, and the world, created according to the divine model, is a web of relationships' (*ibid.*). Further on he adds:

> This leads us not only to marvel at the manifold connections existing among creatures, but also to discover a key to our own fulfilment. The

> human person grows more, matures more, and is sanctified more to the extent that he or she enters into relationships, going out from themselves to live in communion with God, with others and with all creatures (*ibid.*).

We have here a valuable key for understanding much of Beergoglio's teachings, for example, the connection of the environmental with the social, the importance of this latter dimension, his critique of immediate self-reference, etc.

Even more is it the case that 'the Trinity has left its mark on all creation' and a 'trinitarian communion' (*LS*, no. 239), not only creation taken as a whole – as suggested in the previous paragraph – but, as Saint Bonaventure teaches, '*each creature bears in itself a specifically trinitarian structure*' (*ibid.*). Thus he points out to us 'the challenge of trying to read reality in a trinitarian key' (*ibid.*).

At my own risk I would add that it motivates us to interpret each dimension of reality this way as well (ecological, economic, political, cultural, religious, theological). This key helps us to better understand the thinking and action of Bergoglio, and his social ethics.

Part 3

Ecclesial and personal discernment

Chapter 1
DISCERNING GOD'S SIGNS IN PERSONAL AND WORLD HISTORY

This book has primarily followed the golden thread of *mercy*, in order to set out Pope Francis' social ethics, given that it not only expresses the quintessence of the gospel, but characterizes the spirit of his pontificate. As an obvious consequence, we then encounter the *preferential option for and empathy with the poor and vulnerable* precisely in these times of social and ecological crisis and historic shift in the life of humanity. Today there is a real opportunity to overcome the modern technocratic paradigm and try for an alternative globalization for all peoples, following a new model of development and integral ecology for 'all of man and all men,' with a preferential inclusion of the real poor and excluded of today.

In this third part, I will reflect on the *method* which the Pope has been and is still practising, and will explain this approach. I propose to sum it up with the concept and term *discernment* in its Ignatian sense. In the Encyclical *Laudato Si'*, he put it into practice, following the steps which, according to John XXIII (*Mater et Magistra*, no. 236), is the method of the Church's social doctrine: *see, judge, act*, then taken up by Vatican Council II's Pastoral Constitution *Gaudium et Spes*, and by the General Conference of the Latin American and Caribbean bishops at Medellín, Puebla and Aparecida. The concluding document of this last-mentioned Conference was coordinated by the then Cardinal Bergoglio.

In order to set it all out, I will deal first of all with discernment of the *signs of the times* asked of the Church by the Council, understanding them not only as signs of an era, but of God's will in history. In a second step I will cast light on the understanding of this social view by analogy with *Ignatian personal discernment* which Bergoglio himself, following St Ignatius, applies to the social, ecclesial and pastoral scene. In both cases, I will pay special attention to the objective and subjective criteria of discernment, interpreting them, as does Francis himself, from a trinitarian and paschal perspective. Finally, I will present the *four priorities* he expounds as principles of discernment for the social and ethical establishment of a people, the global community of all peoples, and even the People of God in its polyhedric cultural diversity.

1. Ecclesial discernment of the signs of the times

In its Pastoral Constitution *Gaudium et Spes*, after having spoken of the Church's mission at the service of humanity, Vatican II says that to carry out such a task the Church 'has always had the duty of scrutinizing the signs of the times and of interpreting them in the light of the Gospel' (*GS*, no. 4). This is what the Holy Father does in *LS*, and in a number of important sections of *EG* and in *AL* he counsels the faithful, then pastors to do this. It helps him both in governing the Church and guiding the peoples and their governments toward peace, the common good, and integral human development.

However, the Council takes a further step and as a result, so does Francis, when it not only considers the signs that characterize our era in historical and pastoral terms, but discovers in them, in theological terms, the divine *will* in history. Thus Vatican II teaches:

> The People of God believes that it is led by the Lord's Spirit, Who fills the earth. Motivated by this faith, it labors to decipher authentic signs of God's presence and purpose in the happenings, needs and desires in which this People has a part along with other men of our age. For faith throws a new light on everything, manifests God's design for man's total vocation, and thus directs the mind to solutions which are fully human (*GS*, no. 11).

We can underscore significant elements of this text which surely influence the reading the Holy Father makes of it: the Church led by the Spirit of Christ; the faithful People of God as the subject of discernment; the significant role played not only by objective events but also felt needs, feelings, and subjective desires; the text's reference to 'authentic signs', meaning there are also false or *illusory* ones; the reference not merely to Christians but also their contemporaries; and that we can discover – in the light of the gospel as *GS* no. 4 says – God's present action and concrete ends; and finally, that the divine plan 'directs the mind to solutions which are fully human' such that the fact that we go through anti-human or less human situations toward others which are more human, or contrariwise, we go from more human circumstances to one which is a much greater inhuman degradation of circumstances. Over time this has become a very valuable criterion for discernment.

2. *Analogy with Ignatian discernment at a personal level*

My bet is that an improved understanding of Ignatian discernment at a personal level according to Bergoglio, will give us a better understanding of his practice of discernment in governing the Church, his teaching on this in his writings and speeches – especially in his first Encyclical and two Apostolic Exhortations – and the theoretical and practical use of this spiritual procedure in his social ethics, which I dealt with in the first two parts of this work.

To throw light on the Bergoglian understanding of Ignatian discernment, it will help us to read what he wrote in his doctoral notes on Romano Guardini.[1] According to Guardini, each individual receives at birth a word of his or her own which identifies them and serves as an order (*Passwort*) for proceeding on life's journey, a 'word' which is both a free gift and a task to be carried out: it condenses each individual's deepest call, the vocation for which he or she has been chosen, their mission in life. It is the 'password'

---

1 Cf. JM BERGOGLIO, *Personal document of 12 July, 1985, 20*, cited by DJ FARES, 'Prefazione. L'arte del guardare il mondo', in: R GUARDINI, '*L'opposizione polare. Saggio per una filosofia del concreto vivente*', *La Civiltà Cattolica – Corriere della Sera*, Rome, 2014, IX-XI.

(*Pass–wort*) which acts as a guide on the journey and the discernment principle for seeking and encountering God's special will in life. According to Guardini, it will be the basis for divine judgement on the Last Day. When we match up with this call, we match up with the Lord and with ourselves, and gain joy, harmony and peace.

As the Son and the Spirit are the 'two hands of the Father', his will for individuals and society is manifested in the *coincidence*, the matching up of the Spirit and Christ, the Spirit at work within hearts with the figure of Christ in the gospel and in history. We are dealing, then, with consonance between the positive *subjective* movements of the *Spirit* (his fruits: love, joy, peace …) and – by contrast with their negative dissonance – feelings and 'things experienced' in the *objective* contemplation of the mysteries of *Christ*, be it directly by reading the Scriptures or by reading the signs of the times, in other words in historical action interpreted as a *text*[2] in the light of these same Scriptures. This reading takes place especially in the light of the Paschal Mystery of the Lord's cross and resurrection, in which newness and life spring from his death and loving surrender. As I will explain in the following section, in *LS*, Francis reads, in the light of this mystery, social situations of the poor in which they await death, desperation and violence but, thanks to the love which 'proves more powerful' (*LS*, no. 149), are given

---

2 On historical action interpreted as text, cf. P Ricoeur, *Du text à l'action*, Seuil, Paris, 1968, and my book, *Discernimiento filosófico de la acción y pasión históricas*, Anthropos – Univ. Iboamericana, Barcelona-Mexico, 2009.

a superabundance of life, hope and peace, as signs of the saving presence of God at work in the community. This is an Easter shaping of events (an excess of life flowing from death) and its fruit is peace.

In neither the individual nor social case are we dealing with an application of casuistry (syllogistic, static, abstract and timeless), mere general rules applied to a simple particular 'case', but with a dynamic, contextualised, historical and spiritual procedure which is open and no less universally valid because of this, even though not with a univocal universality. Instead, it is a situated, analogous one. The Thomist analogy can help us understand this both universal and singular character, as I attempt to present it in my various written works, or as Lorenz Bruno Puntel does in his studies on analogy and historicity according to St Thomas, or again, the Mexican-Dominican philosopher, Mauricio Beuchot in his analogical hermeneutics.[3]

In his personal notes, cited earlier, Bergoglio calls this word an 'existential *kerygma*' (or proclamation), even prior to the gospel, since it is rooted in it and brings it to fullness as redemption does for creation. Commenting on Guardini, he says that life is a succession of encounters, misunderstandings, and re-encounters with this living word: in the encounters (and re-encounters) there is a *con-sonance*

---

3 I refer especially to Chapter 7 of my book, *Religión y nuevo pensamiento*, Anthropos-UAM (Iztapalapa), Barcelona-Mexico 2005; to: LB PUNTEL, *Analogie und Geschichtlichkeit*, Herder, Freiburg-Basel-Wien 1969, takes up once again the Thomist analogy after Kant, Hegel and Heidegger; and to: M BEUCHOT, *Tratado de hermeneútica analógica*, Ítaca, Mexico 1997.

with this word and, as a result, peace and harmony with oneself (and God). In the misunderstandings, though, there is an intimate *dis-sonance*. Bergoglio relates both these to Ignatian consolation and desolation respectively, inasmuch as both are criteria for discernment. In his 'second time for making a correct and good choice of a way of life', Ignatius guides the retreatant's choice of a way of life according to the direction indicated to him by the spiritual experience of consolations and desolations, on a path of gradual inner harmonization while contemplating and imitating the mysteries of Christ's life. This discernment happens when the retreatant feels an affective consonance in faith with the Lord's feelings and attitudes, or those of the Virgin or apostles and saints or, on the contrary, when he experiences dissonance with these. By taking this path he can arrive at a moral certainty regarding the Lord's choice for his life and mission. He can achieve peace of heart by following the meaning and noting the sequence of consolations and desolations. This usually happens in the second, longer 'week' of the exercises (connected with the 'illuminative way') and is confirmed in the third and fourth weeks (Passion and Resurrection), especially the fourth, which corresponds to the 'unitive way'.

What can happen in an instant in the first time of choice (what happened to Paul on the Damascus Road, or to Matthew, according to Ignatius) usually takes place over time in the *subjective* rhythm of consolations and desolations (affective, or good movements of the Holy Spirit of Love, or good movements but of the bad spirit and self-love) interpreted and discerned according to the *objective criterion* which is the Christ of the gospel, the Easter mystery and the Beatitudes. So when one contemplates, one *feels* and *consents* or otherwise, with 'the same mind, having the same love, being in full accord and of one mind' (Phil 2:2) with Christ.

In my opinion, what Ignatius calls 'consolation without a previous cause' corresponds to the existential *kerygma* (already transformed into an evangelical call). It brooks no hesitation, like Paul's call on the Damascus Road, or the 'Come, follow me' which Matthew heard and left everything behind, and which Ignatius posits as examples of the '*first* time (or manner) or choice'. Furthermore, this *kerygma* likewise serves as a guideline for the *second* 'time of choice' through discernment of consolations and desolations experienced subjectively in the objective contemplation of the mysteries of Jesus' life, since, as we said in the previous paragraph, they are rooted in the affective consonances and dissonances with this kerygma or living word. And even though the 'third time' is carried out through reason enlightened by faith, which considers reasons for or against one or other alternative choice, Ignatius finally goes back to the offering made in prayer to God, the choice made rationally, and seeks its affective confirmation in the inner peace and harmony which have made it a steady choice.

However, the divine light and spiritual experience taught Ignatius what Aristotle, even though a pagan philosopher, and modern 'masters of suspicion' had observed regarding the key role of *intuition* compared to the *true* knowledge of reality. In his *Nicomachean Ethics* VI, Chap. 7, the Stagirite assumes intuitive intelligence to be the condition *sine qua non* of knowledge of truth in practical questions like those of ethics and politics, because the inordinate passions confuse reason. As Paul Ricoeur indicates, Marx, like Freud and Nietzsche (masters of suspicion) warned against class interests, the repressed *libido* and the desire for power respectively, so as not to fall into the *illusion* that his is neither a mere error nor a lie consciously directed at others, but an ideology or rationalization, that is, *self-deception* hiding (even to oneself) bad faith. Hence Ignatius proposes that we free ourselves of 'self-love, desire and interests,' stripping ourselves of inordinate attachments in order to be able to know God's will without being deceived in each situation both personal and social.

To explain this wise way of knowing (wisdom or *sapienza*, coming from *sapere*, a word which means having or sensing flavour, taste), Francis twice appeals to the Thomist understanding of *connaturality*, referring it to infused love. Aquinas employs it to mean the loving exercise of the gift of wisdom, whose faculty is the understanding mind in its power to know the truth. When the Pope refers to the religion of the Christian people, he says:

> To understand this reality, we need to approach it with the gaze of the Good Shepherd, who seeks not to judge but to love. Only from the affective connaturality born of love can we appreciate the theological life present in the piety of the Christian peoples, especially among their poor (*EG*, no. 125).

The second text is even richer and more fertile, and refers to something very important in the life of the faithful people, namely, the anointing of the Holy Spirit given through baptism. Thus he says:

> As part of his mysterious love for humanity, God furnishes the totality of the faithful with an instinct of faith – *sensus fidei* – which helps them to discern what is truly of God. The presence of the Spirit gives Christians a certain connaturality with divine realities, and a wisdom which enables them to grasp these realities intuitively even when they lack the wherewithal to give them precise expression (*EG*, no. 119).

We note that it is about a *sapiential* feeling about the faith, so a 'feeling' which is not purely emotional but also intelligent, and which the Holy Father connects explicitly not only with the judgement of discernment, but also with intuition and wisdom. As a consequence, this specific kind of knowing is related to Pascal's 'reasons of the heart', Plato's *thymos* as Ricoeur understands it; with Xavier Zubiri's *sentient* and, as I have already said, with St Thomas' knowledge *through connaturality*. Therefore, it is not only one human faculty we are talking about – reason, will, affectivity or sensitivity – but a faculty of the *heart* understood as the *root* and *centre* of all those things and as their interconnectedness in our case, including the infused virtues thanks to the action of the Holy Spirit.

On the other hand, this paragraph from *EG* connects, without difficulty, with *GS*, no. 11. Both speak explicitly of the Holy Spirit, of discernment and of the Church as subject. And the 'authentic signs of God's presence and purpose' are 'divine realities' which can be known through our connaturality with them in a kind of *'pati divina'* (suffering or being affected by divine things), in an attitude of receiving God's love and, as a consequence, loving God. It is possible both at a social level (the discerning Church) and the personal level, since there is a correspondence of analogy between the two and whose sign in both cases is peace. Not the peace we find in cemeteries but peace in the justice and love which is there in abundance.

What Ignatius teaches about discernment in the personal area can be understood by analogy in the social area as shown, for example, by the phenomena of ideology (mentioned earlier) and utopia typical of the social imagination (and affectivity). Illusions can occur on both levels, false 'consolations under the species of good' which can be discerned because – instead of proceeding from the anti-human to the human and the more human – they surreptitiously end up leading to 'something evil, or distracting, or less good' (*Spiritual Exercises*, 5th rule of the 2nd week), and damaging, which 'weakens the soul or disquiets it,' 'destroying the peace, tranquility and quiet which it had before (*ibid.*). This is not only about inner harmony, but also the lack of social peace, from the family to global society.

3. *Analogical shift from the personal to the social*

These considerations facilitate the transference from exercising discernment at the level of personal history, to the signs of the times at the level of ecclesial and world history, since both follow the same 'existential logic' which translates the rules of discernment of spirits and the structured meditations of the Ignatian exercises. In the first case it can be about the choice of life or future of the retreatant, or, as the Pontiff himself counsels in *AL* for irregular situations – about personal and ecclesial discernment so that people in these situations may find God's will for themselves and their families when it cannot be reduced to some general canonical rule (cf. *AL*, no. 300) given the particular conditioning and circumstances. In the other case it concerns typical situations of an entire era or the general circumstances of a specific time and place which require one to *see* (interpret) and *judge* (discern) in the light of the Gospel, in order to *act* according to God's merciful plan.

Hence, 'love always proves more powerful' (*LS*, no. 149) than sin (personal or structural) both in personal situations and historical and social ones; it is this which signifies God's active presence, when surprisingly, as if 'from above' and in excess, newness and abundance of concord and life arise where discord and death would seem more obvious.

Earlier I pointed to the case of popular movements with their creative character of being 'social poets'. In *LS*, probably recalling his own experience in 'miserable homes' in his archdiocese, Francis *implicitly* makes this analogical transposition when referring to social situations. He says:

> In the unstable neighbourhoods of mega-cities, the daily experience of over-crowding and social anonymity can create a sense of uprootedness

> which spawns antisocial behaviour and violence (*LS*, no. 149).

Then, immediately after invoking the 'more powerful' effects of love he adds:

> Many people in these conditions are able to weave bonds of belonging and togetherness, which convert overcrowding into an experience of community in which the walls of the ego are torn down and the barriers of selfishness overcome. This experience of a communitarian salvation often generates creative ideas for the improvement of a building or a neighbourhood (*ibid.*).

Bergoglio had already *explicitly* made this analogical transfer from the individual to the social, at least in one case when he wrote about the 'union of souls' in the Society of Jesus as a contribution to the Roman magazine, the *Centro Ignaziano di Spiritualità*. At the time, it was a guide to resolving social conflict, drawing his inspiration from the pacification of conflicting feelings in cases of day-to-day conflict. In both cases – social and personal – there is a dialectic of opposites (not of things that are contradictory), of the kind studied by Guardini in his work *Der Gegensatz* (Polar opposition) selected by Bergoglio as the subject of his doctoral thesis. At the two levels – without losing the energy of their tension – a unity of opposites is achieved through a higher synthesis which does not avoid the conflict but nor is it trapped by it. In both, it is unity, peace and harmony which are the criteria for proceeding properly in discernment and in the subsequent resolution. In both, it is the metaphor of the polyhedron which represents unity achieved amid the tension of difference.

Francis quotes St Ignatius in this article when he is talking about union of souls among Jesuits from different nations in conflict. In my opinion, Bergoglio used the same approach as Archbishop of Buenos Aires when he sought consensus in policies at State level between politicians of different parties, Christian or otherwise. Then as Pope he used it, I believe, in his efforts and achievements in international political ethics.

What the Pope says in *AL* no. 296 regarding 'the two ways of thinking which recur throughout Church history: casting off and reinstating,' referring to irregular individual and family situations, can be transferred to the ecclesial attitude of Church groups to other groups in the Church or in society, given that the gospel way of thinking is that of God's compassionate love which seeks to integrate, not separate. It is the attitude of mercy, which the Pope shows in ecumenical and inter-religious relations and with non-believers, without ceasing to severely condemn sins against the common good without condemning the sinner. So it is, that according to this logic of mercy, he unmasks as temptations 'under the species of good' (both at an individual and global historical level), 'spiritual worldliness' (*EG*, nos 93–97), 'ethical systems bereft of kindness' (*EG*, no. 231) and 'intellectual discourse bereft of wisdom' (*ibid.*) since, under the appearance of fulfilling abstract, universal rules, they display a hardness of heart which violates the gospel of mercy. To the contrary, what is spiritual is not worldly, kindness evaluates conditioning which can exonerate, and wisdom bears in mind individual difference.

4. Four principles as criteria for discernment

From the time he was Jesuit Provincial in Argentina, then as a spiritual writer, much later as Archbishop of Buenos Aires, and finally as Pope, Betrgoglio has appealed to four principles to help himself and to help generally in the exercise of discernment. He did so in the 'shared' Encyclical *Lumen Fidei*, but mainly in the Exhortation *EG*, and finally in his Encyclical *LS*, without mentioning many other minor occasions. He developed them especially in a more systematic form as archdiocesan pastor in his address at the Argentinian Bicentenary (2010) and, as universal Pastor, in *EG* (2013). These are complementary efforts rather than just repetition. In the Exhortation he connects them specifically with 'building a people in peace, justice and fraternity' (*EG*, no. 221), including the People of God and its interconnectedness with the different peoples of the earth, relating them to 'constant tensions present in every social reality' (*ibid.*), the sort of tensions he studied in his research into Guardini.

In other written works, I have dedicated myself to studying the origin and sources of these four principles, and to explaining them in more detail.[1] Here I will simply list

1 See Chapter 11 of my book cited in note 2 of the current chapter.

them and try to show their value for discernment. They are as follows: 1) 'Time is greater than space' (*EG*, nos 222–225); 2) 'Unity prevails over conflict' (*EG*, nos 226–230): 3) 'Realities are more important than ideas' (*EG*, nos 231–233); 4) 'The whole is greater than the part' (*EG*, nos 234–237).

4.1 Time and space

At first sight, it does not seem clear what Francis means when he speaks of the priority of the former over the latter. However, the argument becomes clear when he specifies that he is concerned with *initiating processes rather than possessing spaces* of power (*EG*, no. 223) or in other words, 'generating *processes of people-building*' as opposed to 'obtaining immediate results which yield easy, quick, short-term political gains, but *do not enhance human fullness*' (*EG*, no. 224). In alluding to this positive 'construction' he is spelling out a clear criterion for discernment in opposing sociopolitical praxis, since he is favouring:

> actions which generate new processes in society
> and engage other persons and groups who can
> develop them to the point where they bear fruit
> in significant historical events (*EG*, no. 223).

We observe that it is about 'generating new processes' of a 'people-building' kind, and 'human fullness', but those who initiate them should not control them as an exercise of power. They are to 'engage other persons and groups' which are frequently unpredictable because they are free. The results come with the passing of time. In my opinion it is what Francis is doing to achieve reform both in the Church and in global society: 'Engage other persons and groups' which he cannot control from spaces of power, but who freely follow his renewing initiative and share in his own general evangelizing and humanizing guidance, though in unpredictable ways.

He himself appeals once more to Guardini in searching for a guideline for historical discernment of the times, quoting the German thinker's words:

> 'The only measure for properly evaluating an age is to ask to what extent it fosters the development and attainment of a full and authentically meaningful human existence, in accordance with the peculiar character and capacities of that age' (*EG*, no. 224).

We note that the application of this 'standard' of discernment of an age – ours, for example – takes place within the 'tension between fullness and limitation' (*EG*, no. 222). The guideline fosters human fullness, yet it is historically conditioned by the limitations manifested in the 'peculiar character' which characterizes a particular age, as well as by what is actually *possible* within it. This text connects with what the Pope says much later about discernment of irregular situations in Chapter 8 of *AL*: the criterion is the fullness of marriage and family according to the gospel, but taking into account the situational possibilities given the conditions which impose limits.

Besides, the prioritization of time implies a fundamental change of attitude in the one discerning, at both the sociopolitical and pastoral levels since, besides demanding 'clear convictions and tenacity' (*EG*, no. 223):

> this principle allows us to work slowly but surely, without being obsessed with immediate results. It helps us patiently to endure difficult and adverse situations, or inevitable changes in our plans (*ibid.*).

On the contrary, favouring possession of spaces of power will lead to the ideological absolutization of our own plans and ideas, despite the situation around us counselling otherwise.

Much later, in *LS*, this principle helps the Pope discern, on the one hand, 'a politics concerned with immediate results' (*LS*, no. 178) and 'the myopia of power politics' and, on the other hand, 'true statecraft ... when ... we uphold high principles and think of the long-term common good' (*ibid.*). Hence time (long-term) prevails over space (power-building).

4.2 Unity prevails over conflict

Earlier, when presenting the analogical *transfer* of the personal to the social, I touched on this principle as Bergoglio himself developed it in relation to the 'union (community) of souls', following St Ignatius. Here, I only want to have this principle seen as a criterion for discernment. Francis calls it a 'principle drawn from the Gospel' (*EG*, no. 229), basing it in the unity of everything by and for Christ, and warning us that 'the sign of this unity and reconciliation of all things in him is peace. Christ "is our peace" (Eph s:14)' (*ibid.*). Once again, he explicitly makes the *transfer* we have mentioned, spelling it out as 'the harmonization of diversity' in society 'through conversion of hearts' (*ibid.*), something that happens within.

So, underlying conflict (personal or social) and remaining trapped in it is not resolved but prolonged, and even worsens the dissonances (personal or social) it provokes, even to the point of a fight to the death, at least symbolically. Whereas consonance – both inner and public – reaches out 'for a resolution which takes place on a higher plane and preserves what is valid and useful on both sides' (*EG*, no. 228). It is achieved when conflict is *taken on*, the willingness to 'face conflict head on, to resolve it and to make it a link in the chain of a new process' (*EG*, no. 227). These three last verbs are important for understanding the spiritual workings of the principle.

'Facing conflict head on' is developed through what the Pope says regarding the fact that ' the Lord has overcome the world and its constant conflict "by making peace through the blood of his cross" (Col 1:20)' (*EG*, no. 129). It reminds us of the theory of René Girard that Christ redeems violence by facing up to it. Each of the opposing poles in conflict takes responsibility and overcomes it when each renounces their own absolute position and recognizes the truth of the other's position. 'Resolving it' presumes the willingness to 'go beyond the surface of the conflict and to see others in their deepest dignity' (*EG*, no. 228). It brings us back to what has been said about 'resolution on a higher plane' and to what the Holy Father recognizes further on, that 'the unity brought by the Spirit can harmonize every diversity. It overcomes every conflict by creating a new and promising synthesis' (*EG*, no. 230).

Finally, '*making it a link* in the chain of a new process.' Another translation could say 'transforming it …', taking on a new form where each pole, instead of taking an absolute position, interconnects with others in a multipolar tension of 'communion amid disagreement,' 'a life setting where conflicts, tensions and oppositions can achieve a diversified and life-giving unity' (*EG*, no. 228). We recall Guardini's polar opposites and their role in creating life.

Finally, we note that in this rich text there is a glimpse of a crossover between this second principle and the first one on the priority of time and new processes, and also with the fourth in reference to the whole (considered as a polyhedron) being greater than the part or the mere sum of the parts.

As I have already said many times, the fruit and criterion of good discernment is peace conferred – through the mediation of the cross and the paschal reconciliation in Christ – by the Spirit who, as has been said, 'harmonizes every diversity'. So beauty crowns, confirms and is superabundant in this harmony, since 'diversity is a beautiful thing when it can constantly enter into a process of reconciliation' (*EG*, no. 230). Hence we are talking about a 'reconciled diversity' (*ibid.*).

Later, the Pope applies this principle in *LS* to judge the situation when recommending interdisciplinary and political dialogue between politics and the economy, given that these 'tend to blame each other when it comes to poverty and environmental degradation' (*LS*, no. 198). Unity in dialogue is greater, moves on a higher plane than the conflict of mutual accusation.

4.3 Realities are more important than ideas

'Ideas – conceptual elaborations – are at the service of communication, understanding, and praxis' (*EG*, no. 232), Francis reflects, but since the elaborations are human ones, we need to discern their opposition to what is real. He calls this 'the principle of reality' (*EG*, no. 233). We need to avoid ideas becoming 'detached from reality' (*EG*, no. 231), because they can distort it or mask it instead of showing it. Among the 'various means of masking reality' (*ibid.*) the Pope lists the following:

> angelic forms of purity, dictatorships of relativism, empty rhetoric, objectives more ideal than real, brands of ahistorical fundamentalism, ethical systems bereft of kindness, intellectual discourse bereft of wisdom (*ibid.*).

The first thing that draws our attention is that most of these ways of masking the truth are 'isms' of one kind or another, pointing to the *absolutization* of something partial and the consequent reduction of the totality of the real to just one part of it, the only part captured by *that* idea. This is the conversion of ideas into ideologies, what Bernard Lonergan calls 'bias' because it names the conceptual view of a *biased* reality.

We can also note that almost all ways of '*masking* reality' are creating bias insofar as they remain at the merely abstract, formal, ahistoric, 'pure', both in the theoretical order of things (intellectualism) and the practical (ethical systems), and do not descend to discernment of historical ambiguity, nor to the fact that historical content cannot be reduced to total formalization (since both human and divine freedom come into play). In my opinion, these 'isms' work according to the same casuistic, rigorist, formal, univocal and ahistorical modes of thinking which the Pope rejects in *AL*. As I said much earlier, 'ethical systems bereft of kindness' and 'intellectual discourse bereft of wisdom' are so because there is no genuine ethics, much less Christian ethics, without kindness, and there is no proper understanding of reality without wisdom. Hence the need for this kindness and wisdom to know and judge what is genuinely real according to the gospel.

Then, in his first Encyclical Francis explicitly applies this principle when he critiques the fragmentation of knowledge due to 'the specialization which belongs to technology' (*LS*, no. 110), and the partial views of the different sciences on 'the more complex problems of today's world, particularly those regarding the environment and the poor' (*ibid.*). In turn, he is implicitly employing the fourth principle for discernment, on the priority of the whole over the part and over the mere sum of the parts.

4.4 The whole is greater than the part (and the mere sum of its parts)

Something conceived of in biased form is partial, just as is the affirming of only one of the poles in a conflict.

For Bergoglio, the priority of time is connected with final fullness as opposed to limitations. The other three principles lead to what we are now about to present. In its relationship with discernment, it could be described as the criterion of *differentiated totality*.

Although Francis locates it within the tension between globalization and localization (cf. *EG*, no. 234), I consider it to be a more inclusive criterion, since it extends to *every* kind of totality, distinguishing the uniform (and homogenous) from the multiform (differentiated), in order to cast aside the former and promote the latter. With a view to understanding both better, and then using this distinction as a guide to personal and historic discernment, we are very much assisted by the comparison of the two *models* or geometric figures the Pope offers us as examples:

> Here our model is not the sphere, which is no greater than its parts, where every point is equidistant from the centre and there are no differences between them. Instead it is the polyhedron, which reflects the convergence of all its parts, each of which preserves its distinctiveness (*EG*, no. 236).

The figure of the polyhedron respects the differences which, however, are preserved as they are but are transformed by being raised to a higher plane of a new, richer, more harmonious and diverse totality, like in an orchestra, where the different musical instruments have their unique differences but each with its own sound forms a synthesis, a whole.

This model serves in turn as a criterion for discernment and a guide for action, as the Holy Father observes: 'Pastoral and political activity alike seek to gather in this polyhedron the best of each' (*ibid.*) so that 'even people who could be considered dubious on account of their errors have something to offer which must not be overlooked' (*ibid.*).

Therefore, the image of the polyhedron serves as a guideline for judging not only pastoral practice of and in a Church which is one, but in many senses also diverse, but also political practice (local, national, international, global) according to God's plan, allowing Francis to conclude:

> It is the convergence of peoples who, within the universal order, maintain their own individuality; it is the sum total of persons within a society which pursues the common good, which truly has a place for everyone (*ibid.*).

I think this geometric figure contributes to a better understanding of what 'common good', 'social peace' and 'people' mean for the Pope's social ethics.

Francis finds other examples in the 'integrity of the Gospel which the Church passes down to us and sends us forth to proclaim' (*EG*, no. 237), and in 'the genius of each people' which 'recevies in its own way the entire Gospel and embodies it in expressions of prayer, fraternity, justice, struggle and celebration' (*ibid.*), in other words, he encompasses in a harmonic unity the totality of Christian life in both its contemplative and active aspects.

Later, in *LS*, the Pontiff uses this principle as a criterion for discernment in order to judge the reality and transform it, when he observes that we must not take a partial view by separating the social from the environmental crisis, but see them as a single whole in all its complexity (cf. *LS*, no. 139), since 'there is an interrelation between ecosystems, and between the various spheres of social interaction' (*LS*, no. 141). The whole, and our vision of the whole, prevails over its parts and any partial focus.

4.5 Toward a succinct view of the four principles

Just as, at the level of thought, Bergoglio provides a framework for the oppositions which Guardini speaks of, I believe it is also possible to sum them up at the emotional and imaginative level in the figure of the polyhedron. In fact, he employs it to imagine the whole/part polarity, and it can easily be applied to the overcoming of the unity/conflict opposition on a higher plane; likewise for the tension between reality (whole)/idea (part). I consider that the whole-part dialectic likewise occurs in the pre-eminence of time over space, insofar as the former evokes a diachronic totality open to the latter:

> Broadly speaking, 'time' has to do with fullness as an expression of the horizon which constantly opens before us ... [It is the] brighter horizon of the utopian future as the final cause which draws us to itself (*EG*, no. 222).

On the other hand, 'each individual moment has to do with limitation as an expression of closure' (*ibid,*).

Therefore, the four principles reject – each in its own area – any partial absolutizing (of a part, an idea, a pole, a space) which denies the interrelatedness in the living tension of the opposites.

At the root of this thinking of Guardini's on opposites (not contradictions as in Hegel or Marx) lies Christ explicitly as the living Concrete (*Konkretlebendiges*) in the unity of unconfused and undivided opposites: God/man; and in my opinion, also the tension between identity/difference or unity/plurality as happens, originally, in the Triune God.

As I have suggested earlier, the discernment of the Father's will, personally, ecclesially and socially, comes about through concordance and consonance between his 'two hands' – the Son and the Holy Spirit – or in other words, between the figure (trinitarian, incarnational, paschal, eucharistic) of Christ in personal or social objective reality which is interpreted and judged and, on the other hand, the subjective feeling and sentiment (*Stimmung*) guided by the Spirit, whose signs are harmony and peace (personal and/or social).

www.ingramcontent.com/pod-product-compliance
Lightning Source LLC
Chambersburg PA
CBHW052026290426
44112CB00014B/2399